# Dictator

PHILIP TERRY was born in Belfast and has taught at the universities of Caen, Plymouth and Essex, where he is currently Director of the Centre for Creative Writing. His books include the anthology of short stories, *Ovid Metamorphosed* (2000), the poetry collections *Oulipoems* (2006), *Oulipoems 2* (2009) and *Shakespeare's Sonnets* (2011), and the novel *tapestry* (2013), which was shortlisted for the Goldsmiths Prize. He is the translator of Raymond Queneau's *Elementary Morality* (2007), and Georges Perec's *I Remember* (2014). *Dante's Inferno*, which relocates Dante's poem to current-day Essex, was published in 2014 and was an *Independent* poetry title of the year.

PHILIP TERRY

# DICTATOR

*Carcanet Classics*

MMXVIII

ACKNOWLEDGEMENTS

Thanks to the editors of *para-text* and *Shearsman* magazine, where selections from the poem, in slightly different form, were published for the first time.

C △ R C △ N E T

First published in Great Britain in 2018 by
Carcanet
Alliance House, 30 Cross Street
Manchester M2 7AQ
www.carcanet.co.uk

A CIP catalogue record for this book is
available from the British Library,
ISBN 978 1 78410 618 8

MIX
Paper from
responsible sources
FSC® C014540

Typeset by Andrew Latimer in Joanna Nova
Printed in Great Britain by SRP Ltd, Exeter, Devon

The publisher acknowledges financial
assistance from Arts Council England.

Supported using public funding by
**ARTS COUNCIL
ENGLAND**

# Contents

Stone I Cut i                                                    11

Stone I Cut ii                                                   14

Stone I Cut iii                                                  18

Stone I Cut iv                                                   21

Stone I Cut v                                                    24

Stone I Cut vi                                                   27


Stone II Cut i [Damaged by fire]                                 29

Stone II Cut ii                                                  30

Stone II Cut iii [Beginning damaged]                             33

Stone II Cut iv [End damaged by building work]                   34

Stone II Cut v [End missing]                                     36

Stone II Cut vi [Damaged]                                        38


Stone III Cut i                                                  40

Stone III Cut ii [End damaged]                                   42

Stone III Cut iii [Bomb damage]                                  44

Stone III Cut iv [Beginning damaged]                             46

Stone III Cut v [Damaged by fire]                                48

Stone III Cut vi [Part damaged by fire]                          50


Stone IV Cut I [Part flood damaged]                              52

Stone IV Cut ii [Completely missing or damaged]                  53

Stone IV Cut iii [Completely missing or damaged]                 54

Stone IV Cut iv [Completely missing or damaged]                  55

Stone IV Cut v [Part bomb damaged]                               56

Stone IV Cut vi [Part damaged by fire]                           58

Stone V Cut i [Part damaged by fire]     60

Stone V Cut ii [Part bomb damaged]     62

Stone V Cut iii [Beginning damaged]     64

Stone V Cut iv [End damaged]     66

Stone V Cut v [Damaged by fire]     68

Stone V Cut vi [Damaged by fire]     69

Stone VI Cut i     71

Stone VI Cut ii [Beginning damaged]     73

Stone VI Cut iii     76

Stone VI Cut iv     79

Stone VI Cut v     81

Stone VI Cut vi     83

Stone VII Cut i     84

Stone VII Cut ii     86

Stone VII Cut iii     89

Stone VII Cut iv     92

Stone VII Cut v [Badly flood damaged]     95

Stone VII Cut vi     96

Stone VIII Cut i     98

Stone VIII Cut ii     100

Stone VIII Cut iii [End damaged]     102

Stone VIII Cut iv [Bomb damaged]     103

Stone VIII Cut v [Bomb damaged]     104

Stone VIII Cut vi [Completely missing or damaged]     105

Stone IX Cut i [End damaged]     106

Stone IX Cut ii [End damaged by building work]     108

Stone IX Cut iii [Beginning and end missing]      110
Stone IX Cut iv      112
Stone IX Cut v      113
Stone IX Cut vi [Damaged by flood]      115

Stone X Cut i      116
Stone X Cut ii      119
Stone X Cut iii      122
Stone X Cut iv [End damaged]      125
Stone X Cut v      128
Stone X Cut vi [Beginning damaged]      131

Stone XI Cut I      133
Stone XI Cut ii      136
Stone XI Cut iii      139
Stone XI Cut iv      142
Stone XI Cut v      147
Stone XI Cut vi      150

Stone XII Cut i      154
Stone XII Cut ii      156
Stone XII Cut iii      158
Stone XII Cut iv      161
Stone XII Cut v [Fire damage]      163
Stone XII Cut vi      164

Key      166
Afterword      167

# Dictator

## Stone I Cut i

I will | sing of | the one | who see | the bot | tom…
of he | who know | all I | will tell | the… | story
+ + + in | ~~the old~~ | way… | from be | ginning | to end
+ + +  the | wise ~~one~~ | he who | know ev | ery | thing DIC | TATOR
who see | the sec | ret thing | that no | man see | before
open | the sec | ret place | that no | man op | en be | fore…
and bring | back word | of the | time be | fore the | great wave* –

*see Stone XI

he tra | vel the | … long | road tired | out in | pain + + +
and cut | he work | in stone


He build | the… | strong wall | of big | city | of the | ani | mal noise
the wall | of the | holy | church of | the wo | man ~~sex~~ | ~~god~~ place | of
    peace
Look hard | at… | the wall | the top | be like | steel…
Exam | ine the | in side | wall which | no town | can eq | ual + + +
Touch the | stone door | frame old | as the | mountain
come near | the ho | ly church | home of | the wo | man sex | god + + +
a build | ing… | no dic | tator | can match | to this |  + + + day
Climb the | wall of | big ci | ty of | the an | imal | noise + + +
take a | walk round | the top
exam | ine… | the base | look at | the per | fect brick | work straight |
    and true

Clock that | even | the cen | tre is | of good | fire brick
As for | the base | be it | not set | + + + down | by a | wise man?
One part | be ci | ty one | part fruit | tree one | part ~~mine~~
Three part | togeth | er with | the mine | make up | big ci | ty of | the
    an | imal | noise…


Find the | metal | box full | of cut | stone + + +
slide op | en the | steel lock
… lift | the catch | that hold | the + + + | secret
Take out | the blue | stone and | read it | out loud
How DIC | TATOR | suffer | every | hard ship
over | power | the en | emy | the pow | er full | other
strong one | child of | big ci | ty of | the an | imal | noise pow | er full
    | man cow
He stand | in the | front like | a fear | less man
He march | at the | back as | a + + + | brother
a nuc | lear | weapon | to pro | tect the | army
He be | the great | wave that | break down | the wall
Son of | big ci | ty of | the an | imal | noise…
… DIC | TATOR | … the | blue print | of pow | er…
child of | + + + WILD | COW he | mother
… DIC | TATOR | beauti | ful like | a jew | el in | the dark


He op | en the | mountain | pass…
dig the | deep well | on the | mountain | side…
build the | power | full rock | et…
he tra | vel a | cross the | + + + sea | to where | the sun | god rise
travel | to the | very | edge of | the world | to find | the sec | ret of |
    life…

he find | a way | to the | ONE WHO | FIND LIFE | the one | off
   + + + | the map
the man | who bring | back life | when the | great wave | destroy | it…
+ + + fill | the land | again | with pe | ople + + +

From the | day of | he birth | they call | DICTA | TOR by | name…
DICTA | TOR DIC | TATOR
Be there | a man | like he | … an | y where?
Who like | DICTA | TOR  can | ~~say~~ + + + | 'I am | all pow | er full!'

## Stone I Cut ii

Two part | of he | be god | one part | man + + +
The wo | man sex | god de | sign* (?) the | form of | he bo | dy…

*or 'shape'

She give | to ~~he~~ | …… | ever | y gift
+ + + + + + + + + + + + + + + + + + +
+ + + + + + + + + + + + + + + + + + +
Over | big ci | ty of | the an | imal | noise he | turn he | eye + + +
like a | wild man | cow that | stand tall | head held | … high
When he | fire he | rocket | he have | no eq | ual…
Then the | enem | y burn | + + + + + +
he peo | ple a | wake to | battle | noise + + +
DICTA | TOR take | the son | from + + + | the fat | her… | and beat |
    he…
Through the | ~~holy~~ | place he | run wild | with all | the young | blade
    of | the ci | ty…
+ + + day | and night | he make | the weak | suffer
+ + + day | and night | he tor | ture he | enem | my + + +
+ + + day | and night | he ag | ent hunt | down… | the ref | ugee | who
    come | to the city | for shel | ter + + +
+ + + day | and night | he sec | urit | y pol | ice beat | the ref | ugee | in
    the | prison | behind | closed door
DICTA | TOR who | govern | over | + + + big | city | of the | ani |
    mal noise
Be this | ~~the one~~ | we want | to lead | us strong | bright full | of wis |
    dom…?
DICTA | TOR for | bid the | + + + young | woman | to go | to the |
    mother

the girl | to the | ~~one she~~ | love + + + | the young | woman | to the |
    husband
he get | with the | young wife | before | she hus | band + + +

The… | god hear | the cry
the + + + | god of | the ab | ove [speak | to] AN | + + + the | sky god |
    who pro | tect the | city

'Is it | you that | make this | wild + + + | mighty | man cow?
When he | fire he | … rock | et he | have no | equal
Then the | enem | y burn | + + + + + +
he peo | ple a | wake to |  + + + bat | tle noise
DICTA | TOR + + + | take the | son from | the fat | her and | beat he
+ + + day | and night | he tor | ture he | enem | my + + + | with wat | er
    board
+ + + day | and night | he ag | ent hunt | down… | the ref | ugee | who
    come | to the | city | for shel | ter + + +
+ + + day | and night | he sec | urit | y pol | ice beat | the ref | ugee | in
    the | prison | behind | closed door
Be this | the man | to ~~gov~~ | ~~ern big~~ | ~~city~~ | of the | ani | mal noise?
Be this | the one | to lead | ~~the peo~~ | ~~ple~~…
strong + + + | bright full | of wis | dom…?
DICTA | TOR + + + | forbid | the young | woman | to go | to the |
    mother
the girl | to the | one she | love + + + | the young | woman | to the |
    husband
he get | with the | young wife | before | she hus | band + + +'

When [the | sky god] | AN hear | the peo | ple cry
he call | to the | GREAT MOTH | ER 'You | mother | who cre | ate man

create | now a | second | DICTA | TOR may | they be | … eq | ual*(?) in | spirit | and heart                          *or 'opposite'
May they | fight a | gainst each | other | so that | big ci | ty of | the an | imal | noise may | have qui | et…'


When the | ~~GREAT~~ MOTH | ER hear | this she | make a | + + + ~~pic~~ | ~~ture~~ of | AN + + + | the sky | god in | she heart
Then the | GREAT MOTH | ER wash | she hand | take up | a ball | of wet | earth and | throw it | in to | the wild
In the | wild she | make WILD | MAN the | battle | fit she | give birth | in dark | and si | lence to | one like | the god | of war
He whole | body | be cov | er with | thick hair | he head | be cov | er with | hair like | a… | ~~woman~~
the lock | of he | hair grow | fast and | thick like | the hair | of the | woman | corn god
He know | neither | famil | y + + + | or home | land + + + | he dress | like the | cow god
He feed | with the | wild horse | on grass
with the | ~~wild an~~ | ~~imal~~ | ~~he~~ drink | + + + at | the wa | ter hole
with the | busy | ani | mal he | heart grow | light in | the wa | ter…


The man | who hunt | and kill | … an | imal | CATCATCH
meet he | at the | + + + wa | ter hole
one day | a sec | ond… | and then | … a | third day | + + + he | come ac | ross WILD | MAN at | the wa | ter hole
when he | see WILD | MAN he | body | freeze…
when he | see WILD | MAN he | hand freeze
when he | see WILD | MAN he | eye freeze
WILDMAN | and he | ani | mal to | gether | make the | thing that | be not | welcome

+ + + CAT | CATCH sense | trouble | he wo | rry he | go… | quiet
he heart | ~~hurt~~ + + + | he face | grow dark
The sad | thing en | ter he | heart…
He face | be like | that of | a man | who tra | vel a | long road | at night

## Stone I Cut iii

CATCATCH | shape he | mouth and | move he | tongue to | speak…
… he | say to | he fat | her…
'Father | + + + + + + | a man |  + + + come | from the | mountain
In strength | no one | in all | the land | can eq | ual he
He pow | er be | like a |  + + + bat | tle star (?)* | of AN | … the | sky god

*or 'army'

All day | and ~~night~~ | he go | about | the moun | tain…
all day | and night | he + + + | + + + climb | among | the tree
all day | and night | he feed | on… | grass with | the an | imal
all day | and night | he leave | foot print | and foot | print round | the
    deep | water | hole…
Out of | fear I | can not | go up | to he
He fill | up + + + | the hole | I dig | with I | hand…
he tear | out + + + | + + + the | ~~trip wire~~ | I fix
he help | the an | imal | slip through | I fin | ger + + +
he help | the cat | return | to the | forest
I can | not hunt | in the | wild ei | ther day | or night'


The fat | her shape | he mouth | and move | he tongue | to speak
… he | say to | CATCATCH
'Son… | … in | big ci | ty of | the an | imal | noise…
… there | live a | power | full… | man they | call DIC | TATOR
In strength | no one | in all | the land | can eq | ual he
He pow | er be | like a |  + + + bat | tle star (?) | of the | sky god
Go… | follow | the road | sign in | the di | rection
of big | city | of the | ani | mal noise
May he | who know | all give | you an | ear…

He will | say "Go | CATCATCH | and take | with you | a ho | tel girl |
    … a | top shelf | woman
[she will | win WILD | MAN… | with girl] | power | … pow | er [eq |
    ual and | oppo | site to | he own]
When he | take he | ani | mal to | the wa | ter hole
have the | woman | take off | she skirt
have the | woman | take off | she silk | shirt + + +
have the | woman | + + + show | how beau | tiful | she be
When he | see her | open | she leg | he will | come near
The an | imal | from the | wild… | will run | away | and des | ert he'''

All ear | CATCATCH | listen | to the | word of | he fat | her…
And so | he set | off to | find DIC | TATOR
He climb | the hill | and fol | low the | road sign
in the | direc | tion of | big ci | ty of | the an | imal | noise…
[to speak | to] DIC | TATOR | … the | big head

'+ + + + + + | a wild | + + + man | come from | the ~~moun~~ | ~~tain~~…
In strength | no one | in all | the land | can eq | ual he
He pow | er be | like + + + | the bat | tle star (?) | of AN | + + + the |
    sky god
All day | and night | he go | about | the moun | tain…
All day | and night | he + + + | + + + climb | [among | the tree]
all day | and night | he feed | on… | grass with | the an | imal
all day | and night | he leave | foot print | and foot | print round | the
    deep | water | hole + + +
Out of | fear I | … can | not go | up to | he…
He + + + | fill up | the hole | I dig | with I | hand…
He ~~tear~~ | ~~out~~ the | trip wire | I fix | in the | earth + + +
he help | the an | imal | slip through | I… | finger

he help | the wild | cat re | turn to | the for | est…
I can | not hunt | in the | wild ei | ther day | or night'

DICTA | TOR make | of he | mouth a | shape… | … say | to CAT |
    CATCH…
'Go CAT | CATCH and | take with | you a | hotel | girl + + + | a sex |
    worker
When he | take the | ani | mal to | the wa | ter hole
have the | woman | take off | she skirt
have the | + + + wo | man take | off she | silk shirt
have the | woman | show how | beauti | ful she | be…
When he | see her | open | she leg | he… | will come | near…
The an | imal | from the | wild… | will run | away | and des | ert he'

CATCATCH | go he | take with | he a | sex work | er a | top shelf |
    woman
They climb | the… | long road | travel | in to | the wild
On the | third day | in the | wild they | arrive | at the | place + + +
CATCATCH | and the | woman | sit at | the wa | ter hole | and wait |
    like a | camer | a crew
One day | … a | second | day they | sit sil | ent at | the wa | ter hole
Then on | the third | day the | wild an | imal | come to | the wa | ter
    hole | to drink

## Stone I Cut iv

The an | imal | come… | heart light | in the | water
And WILD | MAN son | of the | up land
he who | feed with | the wild | horse on | grass…
he drink | with the | wild an | imal | at the | water | hole…
and with | the crash | of an | imal | against | … an | imal | he heart | grow
    light

The mag | azine | girl see | he the | man ~~be~~ | ~~fore cul~~ | ~~ture~~ + + +
the wild | action | man from | the far | mountain
'Here be | the man | party | girl get | ready | for a | kiss + + +
Open | you leg | show WILD | MAN you | love box
Hold no | thing back | make he | breathe hard
When he | see you | he mouth | will op | en…
Then he | will come | close to | take a | look + + +
Take off | you skirt | so he | can… | screw you
Make this | man be | fore cul | ture know | what a | girl can | do…
The an | imal | who grow | up in | the wild | will run | away | and des |
    ert he
He will | push he | body | in to | you love | box…'

The mag | azine | girl ~~take~~ | ~~off~~ she | pants and | open | she leg | and he |
    strike + + + | like a | thunder | storm + + +
She do | not hold | back she | make he | ~~breathe hard~~
She spread | out she | skirt… | so he | can lie | ~~on top~~
She make | the man | before | culture | know what | a… | woman | can do
He have | + + + + + + | a hard | on + + +
He have | + + + + + + | a sec | ond hard | on + + +

+ + + + + + | + + + + + + | a third | + + + + + + | + + + + + +
He come | all ov | er she | face + + +
+ + + + + + | all ov | er she | + + + hair
+ + + + + + | all ov | er she | breast + + +
Six day | and se | ven night | WILDMAN | ~~screw the~~ | ~~sex girl~~

When WILD | MAN have | enough | of the | top shelf | girl...
he turn | to look | for the | ... an | imal | + + + + + +
When they | see WILD | MAN the | wild horse | run in | a great |
    wheel...
When they | see WILD | MAN the | big cat | run in | to the | forest
And the | wild pig | dig in | the dirt
All... | the an | imal | of the | wild run | away | and des | ert he
WILDMAN | try to | ~~stand up~~ | but he | body | ~~pull back~~
He leg | freeze... | ... he | arm freeze | ... the | ani | mal run | away | +
    + + + + +
from he | like he | some bad | mother | + + + + + +
~~WILDMAN~~ | grow weak | he can | no long | er run | like be | fore...
face it | he can | no long | er ev | en walk | like be | fore + + +
Yet now | he have | the... | ~~big mind~~ | he have | knowledge | like the |
    web...

WILDMAN | turn round | ... ... | he sit | down... | before | the top |
    shelf girl
WILDMAN | ... look | up at | she face | with a | look of | wonder
and as | the sex | girl speak | he give | she an | ear + + +

The wo | man shape | she tongue | to speak | and say | to WILD |
    MAN...
'Now that | you have | become | wise WILD | MAN...

Now that | you have | knowledge | like the | web…
Why should | you tra | vel the | wild with | the an | imal?
Come… | I will | take you | to the | heart of | big ci | ty of | the an |
    imal | noise…
to the | love house | to the | holy | place of | the sky | god AN | + + +
    and | the wo | man sex | god…
where DIC | TATOR | live all | power | full…
and rule | over | he peo | ple with | a rod | of ir | on…
where DIC | TATOR | live all | power | full…
and like | a wild | man cow | stand firm | + + + push | he peo | ple a |
    bout + + +'

She speak | to he | and they | look at | one an | other
One min | ute two | minute | they look | at one | an oth | er + + +
They look | at one | an oth | er and | she un | derstand
that in | he heart | he long | for a | friend + + +
that in | he heart | he long | for a | ~~friend~~ + + + | to love

WILDMAN | make of | he mouth | a shape | and move | he tongue |
    to speak
he say | to the | ~~maga~~ | ~~zine~~ girl
'Come par | ty girl | join with | WILDMAN | [let us | travel]
to the | love house | to the | holy | place of | the sky | god AN | + + +
    and | the wo | man sex | god…
where DIC | TATOR | live + + + | all pow | er full
and like | a wild | man cow | + + + + + + | + + + push | he peo | ple a |
    bout + + +
I will | call out | to DIC | TATOR | I… | will shout | with nuc | lear |
    force…'

## Stone I Cut v

'I will | cry out | in big | city | of the | ani | mal noise | for all | to ear
"I be | the all | power | full mo | ther...
I be | the bill | ion doll | ar man | here...
I be | the mus | cle man | from the | mountain
I be | the one | who change | ~~judge~~ and | jury
born in | the wild | great might | be mine'"

The mag | azine | girl make | of she | mouth a | shape then | move she |
    tongue to | speak...
she say | to DIC | TATOR
['Come then] | so that | he can | see] you | face...
Who ev | er you | wish to | know... | I can | fix it
Come now | WILD MAN | to big | ~~city~~ | ~~of the~~ | ani | mal noise
where peo | ple wear |  + + + cloth | of gold
and ev | ery day | there be | a par | ty...
where the | people | play loud | music
and the | ... mag | azine | ~~woman~~ | put on | the make | up of | the make
    | up art | ist...
and shine | with sex | light full | of ~~sex~~ | ~~fun~~...
At night | she take | the mo | vie star | to bed
WILDMAN | full of |  + + + life
I will | show you | DICTA | TOR the | ~~happy~~ | ~~sad man~~
Look at | he... | up close | look at | he face
Look in | to he | bright eye
the per | fect man |  + + + like | a sex | machine
he whole | body | be full | of sex | light...
he be | too strong | for you

ever | busy | ... ~~day~~ | and night
WILDMAN | be not | full of | anger
Let me | tell you | about | DICTA | TOR...
The god | of law | love DIC | TATOR
The god | of war | love DIC | TATOR
The god | of love | love DIC | TATOR

The sky | god AN | + + + the | storm god | and the | word god | togeth
   | er they | make he | mind ~~el~~ | ~~astic~~
Long be | fore you | come down | from the | up land
in the | heart of | big ci | ty of | the an | imal | noise... | DICTA | TOR
   see | you ~~in~~ | ~~a dream~~'

DICTA | TOR a | wake he | make of | he mouth | a shape
And... | speak to | he moth | er + + + | WILDCOW | to un | derstand |
   the dream
'Mother | last night | I see | a dream
There be | a star | in the | sky...
Like a | battle | star (?) of | the ~~sky~~ | ~~god~~ AN | it fall
I try | to car | ry... | it but | it be | too hea | vy...
I try | to push | it + + + | ~~but I~~ | can not | move it
Big ci | ty of | the an | imal | noise rise | above | ~~it~~...
the peo | ple + + + | gather | round it
the peo | ple feel | it... | touch it | smell it
the man | ~~and man~~ | of the | city | + + + run | to it
the bus | iness | man look | at it
the wea | ther man | look at | it + + +
the sex | worker | look at | it + + +
people | come to | kiss it
I self | I hold | it like | a wife

And with | a fin | al eff | ort I | lift it
and throw | it down | ... at | you foot
and you | say you | be two | of a | kind...'
The moth | er of | DICTA | TOR skill | full wise
who know | ever | y thing | make of | she mouth | a shape | and...|
    speak to | she son
+ + + WILD | COW the | god* (?) wo | man ~~skill~~ | ~~full~~... | wise who |
    know ev | ery thing | speak to | DICTA | TOR...        *or 'good'

'The star | in the | sky be | you friend
like a | battle | star (?) of | AN the | sky god | it fall | on you
you try | to car | ry... | it but | it be | too hea | vy...
you try | to push | it... | but you | can not | move it
like a | ~~wife~~ you | hold it
with a | final | effort
you throw | it down | at I | foot...
and I | see you | be two | of a | kind...'

26   DICTATOR

## Stone I Cut vi

'The dream | say a | power | full man | will come
… a | man ab | le to | save the | life of | a friend
he pow | er… | will be | great in | the land
Like a | battle | star (?) of | AN + + + | the sky | god will | he pow | er
    be
The one | who you | hold close | to you | … like | a wife
He be | the one | who will | save* (?) you         *or 'take leave of'
This be | the bot | tom of | you dream'

A sec | ond time | DICTA | TOR op | en he | mouth and | move he |
    tongue to | … speak | to he | mother
'Mother | I see | a sec | ond dream
A great | + + + steel | blade drop | from the | sky…
on to | the high | way + + + | of big | city | of the | ani | mal noise
The peo | ple ga | ther be | fore it
The peo | ple press | round it
The fruit | seller | the shoe | seller
the en | gineer | the ref | ugee
I lie | down at | you foot
and I | hold it | … like | a wife
so that | you say | we be | two of | a kind'

The moth | er of | DICTA | TOR skill | full bright | who know | all
    thing | open | she mouth | … and | speak to | she child
WILDCOW | the moth | er god (?) | woman | skill full | bright who |
    know all | thing | speak | to DIC | TATOR

'The knife | you see | be a | man + + +
You love | he and | hold he | ... like | a wife
and treat | he as | you eq | ual + + +
Go [find | he] I | say... | this be | a pow | er full | man ab | le to | save
    the | life of | a friend
he pow | er... | will be | great in | the land
Like a | battle | star (?) of | AN + + + | the sky | god he | will... | have
    great | power'

DICTA | TOR op | en he | mouth and | move he | tongue to | ... speak
    | to he | mother
'May this | be a | lucky | day for | DICTA | TOR...
I will | have a | friend... | to give | advice | + + + + + +
I will | go and | I will | find this | man...'

[Even | as WILD | COW read] | he dream
the top | shelf girl | work she | art on | WILDMAN
where they | ... sit | ...... | alone

## Stone II Cut I

+ + + + + + + + + + + + + + + + +
+ + + + + + + + + + +
.................. + + + + +
...... + + + + + +... + + +... + + +
+ + +...... + + +...... + + +
... + + +... + + +... + + +
+ + + + + +...
+ + + + + +
+ + + + + +
\*   \*   \*


[strong] in | ~~defeat~~ | ......
WILDMAN | sit be | fore the | [top shelf | woman]
+ + + make | love to | gether | + + + + + +
WILDMAN | forget | the moun | tain...
+ + + + + + | is hard | + + + + + +
+ + + + + + | ~~the spread~~ | ~~love bird~~ | + + + + + +
... op | en + + +
... + + + + + + + + + +......
............ + + + + + +
...... | like a | garden | ......
... + + + + + + + + + +
+ + + + + + | wild...
... + + + + + + + + + +
...... | wide...
.........................
... up\* (?) | ......

*or 'down'

## Stone II Cut ii

On the | way to | big ci | ty of | the an | imal | noise + + +
WILDMAN | stop + + + | + + + + + +
+ + + + + + + + + + + + + + + + + + + + + + + +
+ + + + + + + + + + + + + + + + + + + + + + + +
For sev | en + + + | day and | seven | + + +  night | ......
he stop | + + + + + + | + + + + + +
he stay | with the | wool peo | ple + + +
the peo | ple of | the sheep | pen + + +
who live | on the | edge of | the val | ley + + +
[who live | on the | edge] of | the moun | tain + + +
+ + + + + + + + + + + + + + + + + +
On + + + | he first | night + + + | + + + + + +
WILDMAN | + + + ear | a long | story | + + + + + +
+ + + + + + + + + + + + + + + + + + +
On + + + | he sec | ond night | + + + + + +
WILDMAN | drink beer | for the | first time
+ + + + + + + + + + + + + + + + + + +
He smile | and start | to sing | + + + + + +
He eye | light up | like a | + + + star
He ear | ear dif | ferent | noise + + + | in the | night...
+ + + + + + + + + + + + + + + + + + +
~~He go~~ | ~~pasty~~ | + + + he | throw up | + + + + + + | + + + + + +
+ + + + + + + + + + + + + + + + + + +
+ + + + + + + + + + + + + +
At night | WILDMAN | protect | the wool | people
... pro | tect the | sheep...
... he | dress in | thick dark | wool...

and walk | about | the moun | tain at | night…
… he | dress in | thick dark | wool…
and walk | about | the val | ley at | night…
+ + + + + + + + + + + +
one night | he catch | and kill | a wild | dog + + +
the next | night he | catch and | kill a | wild cat
then the | wool peo | ple sleep | easy | in they | + + + bed
+ + + + + + + + + + + + + + + + + +
then + + + | + + + + + + | ……
… to | the house | of mus | ic…
… big | city | of the | anim | al noise | ……
… + + + + + + + + +
+ + + + + +………… + + + + +
+ + + + + +……
+ + + + + +… + + + + + +…
+ + + + + +… + + +
… + + +……
…………………………
… + + + + + + + + +
… + + + + + + + + +……
*   *   *


… in | the street | of big | city | of the | ani | mal noise | ……
… he | make a | … show | of pow | er…
he make | a road | block to | stop the | traffic
all the | bus stop
all the | car stop
big ci | ty ~~buil~~ | ~~ding~~ tow | er… | [over | he]…
the peo | ple gath | er [a | bout he]
the art | commi | ttee gath | er [a | bout he]

the mil | itar | y gath | er round | in a | big cir | cle...
the ref | ugee | gather | round he
They ~~kiss~~ | he as | they might | the ~~foot~~ | of a | new born | child ...
From a | long way | a strong | man he | come...
For DIC | TATOR | god like | an eq | ual come

For the | woman | sex god | the bed | [be put | out at | night]...
For the | + + + + + + | the bed | be put | out at | night + + +
at the | door of | the house | of the | father | in law | WILDMAN | ...
    plant | foot and | foot...
He stop | DICTA | TOR at | the door | of the | house of | the fat | her
    in | law...
He stop | DICTA | TOR from | getting | with + + + | the young | wife
    be | fore she | husband
They seize | each oth | er in | the door | way...
they fight | in the | road through | the ci | ty...
they break | the plate | glass win | dow of | the shoe | store + + +
they break | the plate | glass win | dow of | the wine | store + + +
they break | the plate | glass win | dow of | the ba | by store
they break | the plate | glass win | dow of | the Talk | Talk show |
    room + + +
they break | the plate | glass win | dow of | the tra | vel ag | ent and |
    tear the | picture | of the | great moun | tain + + +
[they knock | down part | of] the | city | wall...
so that | the share | price of | brick go | up ov | er night
And let | out a | great cry | over | big ci | ty of | the an | imal | noise...

## Stone II Cut iii

+ + + + + +

............ + + + + + +

+ + +............ + + +

... + + + + + + + + + + + +...

...... + + + + + + + + + + +

......... + + + + + + + + + + + + + +

............ + + + + + + + + + + +......

+ + +

...

+ + + + + +

\*   \*   \*


In the | land DIC | TATOR | be... | ~~nucle~~ | ~~ar~~...

like a | battle | star (?) of | the sky | god AN | ... the | power | of DIC |
    TATOR

...

The moth | er of | DICTA | TOR move | she tongue | and make | ready
    | to speak

say to | DICTA | TOR...

+ + + WILD | COW ~~make~~ | ~~ready~~ | ~~to~~ speak

say to | DICTA | TOR...

'Son... | + + + + + +

make peace | + + + + + + | with WILD | MAN...

forget | the noise | and the | fog of | battle'

# Stone II Cut iv

…

[strong] in | ~~defeat~~ | …… | [WILDMAN]

he … | tie up | he hair | …… | in to | a man | bun + + +

he smile | in to | he phone | and take | a self | ie + + +

+ + + + + + + + + + + + + + + + + +

DICTA | TOR go | up in | to the | gate house

loud [he | speak]…

'WILDMAN | have no | match + + + | in big | city | of the | anim | al
   noise

In the | wild he | be born | no one | can hold | a can | [dle?] to | he…'


WILDMAN | stand still | he ear | the word | of DIC | TATOR

The word | … make | he go | ~~white all~~ | over | + + + he | sit down |
   and cry

he eye | fill [with | tear]…

he arm | go weak | the pow | er bleed | out of | he + + +


They seize | each oth | er with | emo | tion + + +

take each | other | by the | ~~hand like~~ | [brother]

+ + +

WILDMAN | make of | he mouth | a shape | and move | he tongue

to… | speak to | DICTA | TOR…

'[Friend]…'


+ + + + + + + + + + + +……

……… + + + + + + + +

```
+ + + + + + + + + +
+ + + + +
......
+ + + + +
*   *   *
```

# Stone II Cut v

DICTA | TOR… | open | he mouth | to speak | and move | he tongue
He say | to WILD | MAN…
'To pro | tect… | the [for | est]… | and to | frighten
man ~~earth~~ | ~~god~~ com | mand… | TREEGUARD
he shout | be the | storm rain* (?) | he mouth | be fire | he breathe |
    you dead                           *or *'great wave'*
He will | ear the | foot step | of a | young man | walking | … the | road
    [to | the fo | rest]…
he will | ear the | foot step | … of | all who | go up | to the | ~~forest~~
Of all | who see | the big | red sign | that read | PRIVATE | KEEP OUT
To pro | tect… | the [fo | rest] earth | god he | ~~command~~ | to make |
    the peo | ple fear
Who ev | er go | up to | the fo | rest he | will go | weak at | the knee
Let us | go to | the for | est of | the hard | wood tree
Let us | go to | the for | est of | the hard | wood tree | and fight | with
    TREE | GUARD…
Let us | gain con | trol of | the for | est and | set up | in the | hard
    wood | trade + + +'

WILDMAN | … speak | to he | to DIC | TATOR
'Friend… | you speak | + + + + + +
… ~~heart~~ | ……
… you | speak dan | ger…'
+ + + + + + + + + + +
+ + + + + + + + + + + +
+ + + + + + + + +
+ + + + + +

```
+ + + + + +
+ + + + + + + + + + + +
+ + + + + +
+ + + + + +
*   *   *
```

## Stone II Cut vi                                            [Damaged]

*[WILDMAN compares the anger of TREEGUARD to a great wave]*


… [born] | ……
DICTA | TOR [shape | he mouth | to speak | and move | he tongue
he say | to WILD | MAN] + + +
'Friend… | [in I | house]… | no son | be ~~born~~'

WILDMAN | shape he | mouth [and | move he | tongue he | say to |
    DICTA | TOR]…
'Friend… | … who | want to | make child
when the | child may | be like | + + + + + +
TREEGUARD | ……'

DICTA | TOR laugh | at that | he laugh | be like | a hun | dred horse
then he | … [shape | he mouth | and speak
he say | to WILD | MAN] …
'Friend…
  …'
+ + + + + + + + + + +
+ + + + + + + + + + + + + + + + +
+ + + + + + + + + + + + + + + + + +
+ + + + + +
…………………
+ + + + + +
+ + +
*   *   *

WILDMAN | + + + + + + | + + + + + + | move he | tongue | to speak
He say | to DIC | TATOR
'We must | be care | full…
The an | ger of | TREEGUARD | be like | a…
… great | wave…
+ + +  wa | ter…
… pour | over | ……
mix up | the sea | change the | land + + +
… make | war…
mix up | the wa | ter mix | up the | ~~whole~~ world
… who | anger | is the | great wave
Through the | door of | he mouth | you en | ter the | sky…
The ~~moun~~ | ~~tain~~ give | way the | mountain | explode
… he | hide in | the dark | [of the | forest]
Sky and | earth he | make the | whole of | + + + + + +
[He mouth | be the | fire] god | he breathe | you dead'
+ + + + + + + + + + + + + + + + + +
+ + + + + +………… + + + + + + + + + + +
+ + + + + + + + + + + +
+ + + + + + + + + + + +
+ + + + + + + + + + + + + + + + + + +
+ + + + + +………………
……………………………
……………………………
…………………………
+ + + + + +
+ + + + + +
*   *   *

## Stone III Cut i

The old | people | shape they | mouth to | speak and | move they |
    tongue…
they say | to DIC | TATOR | 'You be | strong DIC | TATOR
… but | do not | put all | you trust | in that
Make sure | you eye | be ~~wide~~ | open
Make sure | you ~~blow~~ | be cer | tain…
The one | who walk | in front | protect | he friend
the one | who know | the way | ~~keep he~~ | ~~friend safe~~
WILDMAN | will walk | before | you as | you go
he know | the path | of the | forest | the way | … to | the hard | wood
    tree
He know | battle | under | stand war
WILDMAN | will watch | out for | he friend | make the | path safe
Over | river | and ~~rough~~ | ~~road~~ he | will car | ry you | body
[WILDMAN] | the peo | ple of | the ~~big~~ | ~~city~~ | hand DIC | TATOR |
    over | to you
you in | turn must | bring he | back home | again'

DICTA | TOR op | en he | mouth + + +
He make | of he | mouth a | shape + + +
and speak | to WILD | MAN…
'Get up | + + + bro | ther… | we will | go to | the ho | ly* (?) house

*or 'great'

to see | WILDCOW | + + +  the | great one
WILDCOW | the wise | who know | ever | y thing
She will | map out | a safe | path… | for the | ~~foot and~~ | ~~foot~~…

They hold | each oth | er… | they walk | hand | in hand
DICTA | TOR and | WILDMAN | togeth | er… | go up | to the | holy
    (?) | house…
to see | the wild | cow the | great one | the moth | er…
DICTA | TOR go | near he | enter | the house | of the | wild cow
then op | en he | mouth to | speak…
'WILDCOW | I [want] | + + + + + +
[to tra | vel] a | long way | to the | home of | TREEGUARD
in the | dark heart | of the | forest
[I will | face] a | battle | the out | come of | which I | can not | see
    + + +
I will | … tra | vel a | path I | do not | know…
[until | the time | I re | turn] + + +
[until | I reach | the fo | rest… | of the | hard wood | tree] + + +
until | I gain | control | of the | forest
+ + + and | set up | in the | hard wood | trade + + +
[until | I des | troy TREE | GUARD he | who ex | plode in | you face]
[and re | move from | the land | the ev | il that | the sun | god hate]
… a | ~~coat~~…
+ + + in | you ~~com~~ | ~~pany~~'

… WILD | COW speak | to she | son DIC | TATOR
'… lis | ten + + + | son…
is this | such a | good id | ea…?'

# Stone III Cut ii

WILDCOW | + + + go | in to | [the sec | ret room]
[she wash | she bo | dy] with | … soap
[she put | on a | dress] that | fit like | a bo | dy stock | ing + + +
[she put | a star] | on she | chest…
on she | head + + + | she put | ~~a hat~~ | of gold
She… | the ground | + + + + + + | + + + + + + | ~~sex girl~~
She climb | up the | step go | right… | up to | the roof | ~~garden~~
… on | the roof | garden | she light | a fire | for the | sun god
she make | a ~~sac~~ | ~~rifice~~ | ~~to the~~ | ~~sun god~~ | and lift | up she | arm…

'Why do | you fire | up I | son DIC | TATOR | … and | give he | a heart |
    that will | not rest?
Now you | call on | DICTA | TOR to | travel
a long | road + + + | to the | home of | ~~TREEGUARD~~
to fight | a bat | tle that | he can | not win
and tra | vel a | path that | he can | not know
until | the time | he re | turn… | dead or | alive
[most like | ly dead] | + + + in | a bo | dy bag
until | he reach | … the | forest | of the | ~~hard wood~~ | ~~tree~~ + + +
until | he kill | TREEGUARD | who ex | plode in | you face | with nuc |
    lear | force + + +
and re | move from | the land | the ev | il that | you hate
On the | day set | down as | he last
if he | honour | … ~~you~~ | may you | wife make | you re | member | this
    + + +
and may | she send | he in | peace to | the court | of the | night…'
……………………………

+ + + + + + + + + + + +......
...... + + + + + + + + + + + +......
...................... + + + + + + + + + + +
+ + + + + + + + + + + + + + + + + + + + + + +
..................
+ + + + + +
\* \* \*

## Stone III Cut iii

The liv | ing fear | for DIC | TATOR
The dead | fear for | DICTA | TOR…
The god | and god | fear for | DICTA | TOR…
… + + + + + + + + +
When he | prepare | to leave
The ~~sky~~ | ~~god~~ AN | + + + and | the oth | er + + + | ~~sky god~~ | ……
… + + + + + + + + + +………….
………………………… + + + + + +
The… | traffic | ……
damage* (?) | ……                                      *or 'danger'
because | ……
the road | …… | always | + + + bu | sy + + +
… + + + + + + + + + + + + + + +
until | [DICTA | TOR] reach | the fo | rest and | return | safe + + +
or un | til DIC | TATOR | reach the | forest | and re | turn in | a bo | dy
    bag
in a | [day]…
or a | [month]… | ……
or a | [year]… | ……
… ten | year… | ……
+ + + + + + + + + + + + + + + + + +
+ + + + + + + + + + + + + + + + + +
+ + + + + +
+ + + + + + + + + + +
………………………… + + +

+ + +..........................
...........................
............
.........................................
.........................................
*   *   *

## Stone III Cut iv

\+ + + + + +…………

\+ + + + + + + + +…

\+ + + + + + + + + + + +………… + + + + +

\+ + + + + + + + +… + + + + + +

\+ + +………………… + + + + + + + + + +

\+ + + + + + + + + + + + + + + + + + + + + + +

\+ + + + + + + + + + + + + + + + + + + + + + + + + +

\+ + + + + + + + + + + + + + + + + + + + + + + + + + + + + + + +

…………………………………

\+ + + + + + + + + + +

\+ + + + + + + + + + + +……

…………………

\+ + + + + +

In the | sky the | sun god | call to | the storm

… WILD | MAN make | + + + + + +

\+ + + + + + + + + + + + + + + + +

\+ + + + + + + + + + + + + + + +

… WILD | COW hon | our he | seat he | before | the cam | era

She speak | to WILD | MAN + + + | tell he | the news

'WILDMAN | power | full one | you be | not the | child of | I fam | ily

But now | I ac | cept you | in to | I fam | ily

with the | woman | who hold | the ~~see~~ | ~~ret~~ the | woman | who love |

    DICTA | TOR…

the ho | ly wo | man the | wife of | the big | city | god + + +

the love | girl who | throw a | way care'

She put | a jew | el round | the neck | of WILD | MAN…
The wo | man and | woman | take he
~~the daugh~~ | ~~ter~~ of | the god | make he | + + + hard

'I be | WILDMAN | who come | [to]…
WILDMAN | …… | to…
… make | love…
…'
until | they go | and re | turn un | til they | ~~reach~~ the | forest | of the |
    hard wood | tree + + +
until | they gain | control | of the | forest
or un | til they | reach the | forest | and re | turn in | a bo | dy bag
in a | day + + +
in a | month + + +
or  a | year… | ……

## Stone III Cut v                                    [Damaged by fire]
[DICTATOR and WILDMAN prepare to travel to the forest]


\+ + + + + + + + + + + + + + + + +
\+ + + + + + + + + + +
\+ + +............ + + +
\+ + + + + +
\+ + + + + +
\+ + + + + + + + + + + + + + + + + + + + + + +
\+ + + + + + + + +...... + + +
\+ + +... + + +... + + + + + +
\+ + + + + + + + + + + + + + + +
\+ + + + + + + + + + + + + + + + + + + + + + + +
\+ + + + + + ~~hurt~~...................
.................................
.................................
.................................
.................................
... + + + + + + + + +
\+ + + + + +
\+ + + + + +
\+ + + + + +
\+ + + + + + + + + + + + + + + + + + + + + + + +
\+ + + + + + + + + + +
\+ + + + + +
\+ + + + + +
\*   \*   \*

[until | they go | to the] | ~~hard wood~~ | forest
until | they gain | control | of the | forest

until | they set | up in | the hard | wood trade
[until] | they kill* (?) | [TREEGUARD | the might | y one]

*or [find] 'the hill'
until | they reach | the for | est and | return | in a | body | bag + + +

# Stone III Cut vi

[DICTATOR and WILDMAN leave for the forest]


\+ + + + + + + + + + + + + + + + +

\+ + + + + + + + + + +

\+ + + + + + + + + + + + + + + + +

\+ + + + + + + + + + + + + + + + + + + + + + +

\+ + + + + + + + + + + + + + + + + +

\+ + + + + + + + + + +

\+ + + + + + + + + + + + + + + + +

\+ + + + + + + + + + + + + + + + + + + + +

The old | people | shape they | mouth to | speak and | move they | tongue…

they say | to + + + | WILDMAN

'WILDMAN | will pro | tect he | friend… | guard DIC | TATOR

he will | carry | he bo | dy ov | er ri | ver and | rough road

The peo | ple of | + + + ~~big~~ | ~~city~~ | of the | ani | mal noise | hand DIC | TATOR | over | to you

you in | turn must | bring he | back home | again'


WILDMAN | move he | tongue then | shape he | mouth and | speak…

he say | to DIC | TATOR

'Friend… | … come

the path | + + + + + + | is long

…'


…………………………………

\+ + + + + + + + + + + + + + + + + +

…………………………………

+ + + + + + + + + + + + + + + + + + + + + + + + + + +

...................................................

+ + + + + + + + + + + +

..................

+ + + + + +

.........................................

+ + + + + +

......

+ + + + + +

............

+ + + + + +

*  *  *

## Stone IV Cut I                                    [Part flood damaged]

[DICTATOR and WILDMAN pray to the sun god on the way to the forest]


At twen | ty horse | they break | off for | a smoke

At thir | ty horse | they take | a look | at the | road map

At for | ty horse | they get | ready | for the | night...

At fif | ty horse | they walk | all day | + + + get | sun burn

At six | ty horse | they break | off for | a can | of beer

The dis | tance of | a month | and ten | and five | day they | travel | + + +
    in | three day

+ + + for | the ~~sun~~ | ~~god~~ they | dig a | well + + +

.................................................

+ + + + + + + + + + + + + + + + + +......

....................... + + + + + + + + + + +

+ + + + + + + + + + + + + + + + + + + + +...

+ + + + + + + + + + + + + + + + +

...................................

...................................

+ + + + + +............

...................................

+ + + + + +......

+ + + + +

+ + + + +

+ + +

*   *   *

# Stone IV Cut ii

[DICTATOR dreams of TREEGUARD?]


.................................................
+ + + + + + + + + + + + + + + + + +......
...................... + + + + + + + + + + +
+ + + + + + + + + + + + + + + + +............
+ + + + + + + + + + +...
+ + + + + + + + + + + + + + + + + +
.................................... + + + + + +............
+ + + + + + + + + + + + + + + + + +
....................................
+ + + + + +............
....................................
+ + + + + +...... + + + + + +
+ + + + + +............ + + +...
+ + + + + +... + + +......... + + +
+ + + + + +............
+ + + + + +
+ + + + + +
+ + + + + +............
+ + +
* * *

## Stone IV Cut iii                [Completely missing or damaged]

[They continue on the way to the forest?]


.................... + + +... + + +.........

+ + + + + + + + + + + + + + + + + + +......

... + + +... + + + + + + + + +

+ + + + + + + + + + + + + + + + + +............

+ + + + + + + + + + +...

+ + +... + + + + + + + + + + + +

.................................... + + + + + +............

+ + + + + + + + + + + + + + + + + +

.................................. + + + + + + + +

+ + + + + +............ + + + + + + + + + + +

.................. ~~or~~...... + + + + + + + + +

+ + + + + +...... + + + + + +

+ + + + + +............ + + +...

+ + + + + +... + + +......... + + +

+ + +... + + + + + + + + + + + +

.................................... + + + + + +............

+ + + + + + + + + + + + + + + + + +

.................................. + + + + + + + +

+ + + + + +............

+ + + + + + + + + + +

+ + + + + +

+ + +...... + + +......

+ + +


*   *   *

## Stone IV Cut iv

[They continue on the way?]

[Completely missing or damaged]


\+ + + + + + + +
\+ + + + + + + + + + + + + + + + + +
............... + + + + + + + + +
\+ + + + + +...... + + + + + +
\+ + + + + +............ + + +...
\+ + + + + +... + + +......... + + +
\+ + +... + + + + + +
............ + + + + + +............
\+ + + + + + + + + + + + + + + + + + +
................................ + + +
\+ + + + + +............
\+ + + + + + + + + + +
\+ + + + + +
\+ + +...... + + +......
\+ + +
\*   \*   \*

## Stone IV Cut v

[DICTATOR and WILDMAN prepare to fight TREEGUARD]

+ + + + + + + + + + + + + + +............
+ + + + + + + + + +...
+ + + + + + + + + + + + + + + + +
.................................... + + + + + +.............
+ + + + + + + + + + + + + + + + + + + + + + + + +
.................................... + + + + + +
+ + + + + +............ + + + + + + + + + + +
.................................... + + + + + +
+ + + + + +...... + + + + + +
+ + + + + +............ + + +... + + + + + +
+ + + + + +... + + +......... + + + + + + + + +
+ + + + + +............ + + + + + + + + + + +
+ + +... + + + + + + + + + + + + + + + + + +
+ + + + + +...... + + + + + + + + + + + +
+ + + + + +............ + + + + + +
+ + + + + +
*   *   *


... DIC | TATOR | child of | ... big | city | of the | ani | mal noise
open | he mouth | to speak | and move | he tongue | + + + fill | with
    might
he say | to WILD | MAN...
'Before | + + + in | the heart | of big | city | of the | ani | mal noise |
    you stand | tall + + +
Get up | ... and | go in | to bat | tle [that | you may | kill TREE |
    GUARD...]
Hurry | up jump | to it | do not | give he | a chance | to slip | a way

Go to | the fo | rest of | the hard | wood tree | + + + [do | not have | fear]…

TREEGUARD | + + + have | airplane | with chem | ical | weapon

+ + + [he] | + + + have | ~~heli~~ | ~~copter~~ | with sev | en nuc | lear | war head* (?)                                                                                        *or 'rocket'

One he | get rea | dy six | be not | ready | yet + + +

Like an | anger | wild cow | ……

Once rea | dy he | kill you | ……

TREEGUARD | the law | of the | forest | ~~cry out~~ | ……

TREEGUARD | like…'

# Stone IV Cut vi

[Part damaged by fire]

[They reach the door of the forest]

\+ + + + + + + + + + +
\+ + + + + + + + + + + + + + + + +
\+ + + + + + + + + + + + + + + + +
\+ + + + +
\+ + + + + + + + + + + + + + + + +
\+ + + + + + + + + + + + + + + +
\+ + + + +
....................
\+ + + + +
\+ + +
\*   \*   \*

WILDMAN | shape he | ~~mouth and~~ | move he | tongue to | speak he | say to | DICTA | TOR + + +

'[Man we | must not | climb] up | [in to | the dark | forest] | of the | hard wood

We must | not set | up in | the hard | wood trade

I heart | grow weak | when I | touch... | the door'

DICTA | TOR op | en he | mouth and | move he | tongue he | speak to | WILDMAN | he say

'... Man | like one | who cry\* (?) | when he | remem | ber + + + | the dead           \*or 'go weak'

You must | be strong | + + + + + +

[You] will | out live | + + + all | who come | before | + + + + + +

You be | a man | who ~~un~~ | ~~derstand~~ | battle | + + + who | know how | to fight | with tooth | and nail

Touch [I | heart] + + + | you must | not fear | to die

Let us | shout to | gether | like + + + | hard men | and we | will rise |
    up + + +

like the | beat of | an an | imal | skin stretch | ~~on wood~~ | the shout |
    will tra | vel ac | ross the | mountain

Then the | fear in | you heart | the fear | in you | body | … will | leave
    you

Stand firm | friend we | will [climb | up] to | gether | hand in |
    hand…

May you | heart grow | light in | battle | do not | fear to | die fear | no
    thing

With great | power | the wise | man + + +

go in | front guard | he bo | dy pro | tect he | friend…

Even | though they | fall they | make his | tory'


They come | near to | the [door] | tear op | en the | lock the | two to |
    gether

Still in | silence | they stand | hand in | hand…

they en | ter the | dark of | the for | est…

# Stone V Cut i

[Part damaged by fire]

[DICTATOR and WILDMAN enter the forest]


They stand | and look | at the | forest
They see | the great | height of | the tree | the great | size like | a truck
They see | the dark | go on | for ev | er like | a + + + | bad night
they see | the fo | rest door | the bro | ken lock
Where TREE | GUARD walk | the eye | make out | a path
The way | be straight | the path | good... | + + + for | transport
They see | the ~~tree~~ | ~~mountain~~ | home of | the god | and god | seat of |
    the wo | man sex | god...
In the | heart of | the moun | tain the | tree be | heavy | with fruit
The shade | is good | full of | comfort
The sharp | blade that | hide in | the un | der growth | they see |
    not...
The trip | wire that | lie in | the grass | they see | not + + +
... the smell | of the | tree...
... one | two hour | ...... + + + + + +
... ag | ain for | two hour | ...... + + + + + + + + + + + +
.......................................... + + + + + +
+ + + + + + + + + + + + + + + + + + + + + + + + +
+ + + + + + + + + + + + + + + + + +
...... + + +......................... + + +
.......................................... + + + + + +
+ + + + + + + + +... + + + + + + + + + + + +
+ + + + + + + + + + + + + + + + + + + +...... + + + + + +
...... + + + + + +......................... + + + + + +
.......................................... + + + + + +... + + +
+ + + + + + + + + + + + + + + + + + + + + + + + +

............................. + + + + + + + + + + + + + + + + + +
........................................ + + + + +
+ + + + + + + + + + + + + + + + + + + + + + + + + +
+ + + + + + + + + + + + + + + + + +
.............................. + + + + +
+ + + + + + + + + + +
+ + + + +
* * *

## Stone V Cut ii

[They prepare for battle]


From far | off the | bullet* (?) | …… | fly + + +          *or 'rocket'

power | over | long dis | tance…

…… | touch all | in its | path…

…… | bullet (?) | ……

+ + + + + + + + + + + +

under | cover | + + + + + +

TREEGUARD | + + + + + +

The sign | read DO | NOT EN | TER + + +

The sign | read KEEP | OUT + + +

The sign | read PRI | VATE PROP | ERTY

The sign | read HARD | HAT MUST | BE WORN | AT ALL | TIMES

   + + +

+ + + + + +

+ + + + + + + + + + + +

…………

……………………

……………………

…………

+ + + + + +

The chief | god smile | ……


WILDMAN | make of | he mouth | a shape | and move | he tongue

[he | say] to | DICTA | TOR…

'… kill | ~~TREEGUARD~~ | ……

Alone | we be | weak to | gether | strong…

The land | be for | eign…

The dark | of the | forest | go on | for ev | er…
Separ | ate we | will slip | on the | ground…
Separ | ate we | will step | on the | trip wire
Two… | togeth | er be | strong + + + | like three
~~Like a~~ | ~~rope~~ + + +
Strong [like] | two big | [cat] + + + | three + + + | big cat | ready | for
    the | hunt…

+ + + + + + + + + + + + + + + + + +

+ + + + + + + + + + + + + + + + + +

………………………………………

………………………………………

………………………………………

…………………………………

………………………………

+ + + + + + + + + + +

+ + + + + + + + + + +

+ + + + + + +

+ + + + +

\*   \*   \*

## Stone V Cut iii

[DICTATOR dreams of TREEGUARD and makes an offering to the sun god]


+ + + + + + + + + + + + + + + +

+ + + + + +............ + + + + + + + + + +

+ + + + + + + + + + +

+ + + + + + + + + + +

+ + + + + + + + + + + + + + + + +

+ + + + + +.................

..............................

...................................

...................................

+ + + + + + + + + + +

+ + + + + + + + + + +

\* \* \*

DICTAT | OR make | of he | mouth a | shape and | move he | tongue
   to | speak he | say + + +
'In the | other | dream I | see…
in to | a big | hollow | between | two high | mountain
[a moun | tain] fall | ……
… like | a fly | ……'


The one | born in | the wild
make of | he mouth | a shape | and…
speak to | he friend | WILDMAN | open | the dream
reach in | to the | dream work | + + + + + +
'Friend the | dream be | a sign | of good | luck…
the dream | is ~~gold~~ | …… | the dream | is big | business
the dream | is a | gift of | the god | and god

Friend the | mountain | you see | is the | enem | y…
the moun | tain you | see fall | like a | fly be | TREEGUARD
we will | seize TREE | GUARD and | ~~throw down~~ | he bo | dy…
and he | will lie | flat on | the earth'

On the | … day | after | + + + + + + + + + + + +
At twen | ty horse | they break | off for | a smoke
At thir | ty horse | they take | a look | at the | + + + map
At for | ty horse | they rest | + + + + + +
At fif | ty horse | they break | off for | a can | of beer
for the | sun god | they dig | a hole | in the | ground…
DICTA | TOR stand | over | it…
He throw | ~~food~~ in | to the | hole…
He pour | half he | beer in | to the | hole…

'Mountain | make the | dream live
Do it…'

# Stone V Cut iv

The moun | tain bring | anoth | er dream
In the | night…
a cold | wind come | by…
and make | he lie | down on | the earth
… and | like a | child be | fore birth
DICTA | TOR bring | he leg | up to | he chest
Sleep pour | over* (?) | he gift | of rest          *or 'come over'
Then + + + | in the | middle | of the | night + + + | + + + all | of a |
    sudden | … he | awake
He rise | up and | make of | he mouth | a shape | say to | he friend

'WILDMAN | … you | do not | call… | why then | do I | awake?
You do | not touch | DICTA | TOR… | what then | trouble | he sleep?
No god | pass by | … why | do I | leg turn | to stone?
Friend I | see a | third dream | in the | night + + +
and the | dream I | see be | one that | frighten | I in | every | way + + +
The sky | cry out | the earth | shout + + +
All the | tree cry | out all | the tree | shout + + +
All the | hard wood | tree fall | down + + +
the soil | go all | black + + +
Day light | disap | pear and | ~~dark cov~~ | ~~er all~~
The bat | tle star (?) | of the | sky god | AN + + + | make great | noise
    fire | break out
the rain | cloud make | war the | rain bring | down dead | body
The light | ~~disap~~ | ~~pear~~ + + + | the fire | ~~go out~~
the soil | run with | the wind | + + + + + +

[and all | that] fall | turn to | ash + + +
Let us | go down | to the | valley | and talk | it ov | er…'

When WILD | MAN hear | the dream | he say | to DIC | TATOR
'… the | sun god* (?) | the chief | the one | who cre | ate + + +

                                        *or 'dream work'

……………………………………………………
……………………………………………………
……………………………………………………
……………………………………………………
+ + +… + + + + + + + + + + +
…………………………… + + + + + +…………
+ + + + + + + + + + + + + + + + + +
……………………… + + + + + + + +
+ + + + + +………… + + + + + + + + + + +
+ + + + + + + + + + + + + + + + + +
+ + + + + + + + + + + + + + + + +
+ + +…… + + +…… + + + + + +
+ + + + + + + +
*   *   *

## Stone V Cut v

[They steel each other for the fight]


\+ + + + + + + + + + + + + + + + +
\+ + + + + + + + + + +
.................. + + + + +
...... + + + + + +... + + +... + + +
\+ + +...... + + +...... + + +
... + + +... + + +... + + +
\+ + + + + +...
\+ + +...... + + +...... + + +
... + + +... + + +... + + +
\+ + + + + +...
\+ + + + +
\+ + + + +
\*   \*   \*

... DIC | TATOR | ~~WILDMAN~~ | ......
WILDMAN | shape he | mouth to | speak and | move he | tongue...
... he | say to | DICTA | TOR...
'Friend I | hear... | you and | + + + + + +
to go | down...'

## Stone V Cut vi

[The death of TREEGUARD]


+ + + + + + + + + + + + + + + + +

+ + + + + + + + + + +

................. + + + + +

...... + + + + + +... + + +... + + +

+ + +...... + + +...... + + +

... + + +... + + + + + + + + +... + + +

+ + + + + +... + + + + + + + + + +

+ + +...... + + +...... + + + + + + + +

... + + +... + + +... + + + + + + + +

+ + + + + +... + + + + + + + + + + +

+ + + + + + + + + + +

+ + + + + + + + + + +

*   *   *

They come | to the | path... |  + + + + + +

+ + + a | ~~second~~ | time + + +

The way | be straight | the path | good for | transport

The sign | read KEEP | OUT + + +

The sign | read PRI | VATE PROP | ERTY

The sign | read HARD | HAT MUST | BE WORN | AT ALL | TIMES +

   + +

The sign | read DO | NOT EN | TER + + +

+ + + + + + + + + + +

They en | ter + + + | + + + + + +

+ + + + + + + + + + +

+ + + + + + + + + + +

... WILD | MAN...

... throw | down... | the en | emy

+ + + + + + + + + + + + + + + + + + + + + + + + + + + +

+ + + + + + + + + + + + + + + + + + + + + + +

They cut | off the | head of | TREEGUARD

## Stone VI Cut i


He wash | the dirt | out of | he hair | … and | clean he | ~~behind~~
he shake | out the | lock of | he hair | over | he back
he throw | off he | old shirt | … and | he put | on a | clean one
he put | on a | jacket | ~~fix the~~ | button
DICTA | TOR put | on he | hat of | gold + + +


To beau | tiful | DICTA | TOR the | woman | sex god | turn an | eye…
'Come DIC | TATOR | give I | the fruit | of you | body!
Give I | the taste | of you | perfect | skin…
~~Be I~~ | ~~husband~~ | ~~and I~~ | ~~will be~~ | ~~you wife~~!
I will | give you | a gold | sport car
A car | fit for | a bus | iness | man + + +
A car | fit for | the ow | ner of | the for | est of | the hard | wood tree
With gold | wheel and | a sun | roof…
You will | drive a | fast road | machine | a hot | mother!
Enter | this house | smell the | sweet air
When you | enter | the house
the ho | ly man | will kiss | you foot | + + + as | they do | in the | city |
   of gold
Minis | ter may | or and | gener | al will | bow down | in front | of you
For mon | ey talk | and you | know what | it say
Mountain | and land | will bring | + + + fruit | to you
You an | imal | will have | many | ~~off spring~~
You po | tato | will grow | deep you | corn will | grow high
You horse | will win | the big | race…
You in | vestment | will in | crease + + +
You cow | will pro | duce fine | + + + ~~cheese~~'

DICTA | TOR make | of he | mouth a | shape and | move he | tongue…
He say | to the | woman | sex god
'What can | I give | you if | I take | you for | a wife?
Will I | give you | oil for | the bo | dy… | and cloth | of gold?
Will I | give you | bread and | + + + ~~cheese~~?
you who | eat the | food of | the god
you who | drink wine | fit for | a dip | lomat?
[For you] | they pour | out + + + | [holy | water]
[you dress | in cloth] | of gold
[what] a | distance | between | [you and | DICTA | TOR] if | I take |
    you for | a wife!

You be | a camp | fire that | go out | in the | rain…
a back | door that | ~~shut out~~ | neither | wind + + + | or storm
a base | camp that | kill the | young boy | that de | fend it
a car | with a | door that | fall off
a bomb | that ~~ex~~ | ~~plode~~ in | the hand
a bot | tle that | leak… | over | the one | who drink | from it
stone that | break up | in the | city | wall + + +
a spy | that go | over | to a | foreign | power
a shop | that give | no mon | ey back
a man | who sell | refug | ees in | to the | sex trade
a shoe | that bite | the foot!

Who that | you love | do you | love for | ever?
Which of | you par | ty boy | please you | for long?
Come I | will name | all you | lover | boy + + + | for you'

# Stone VI Cut ii

...........................................
......................................
...............................
.............................

... + + + + + + + +
+ + + + + + + + + + +
+ + + + + + + + + + +
+ + + + +
+ + + + + + + + + + + + + + + + + + + + + +
+ + + + + + + + + +
+ + + + +
+ + + + +
\*   \*   \*

'... the | god of | the ~~cow~~ | ~~man~~ you | love once
you send | he to | visit | the un | der world
Year af | ter year | the peo | ple cry | for he
You love | the dark | ~~cow bird~~
you seize | he and | + + + break | he wing
He stand | in the | forest | and cry | "Come back | wing! Come | back
    wing!"
You love | the big | cat... | ~~full of~~ | ~~strength~~ + + +
you dig | for he | seven | hole and | seven | hole\* in | the ground
                                                              \*many
You love | the war | horse + + + | strong in | battle
you give | he the | bomb + + + | and the | bullet
because | of you | ... he | ~~run for~~ | the hill
because | of you | ... he | hate the | water | he drink

because | of you | he moth | er cry
You love | the cow | man who | work in | the field
who give | you fruit | and bread | to eat
who ev | ery day | kill a | young cow | for you
You strike | he and | turn he | in to | a + + + | wild dog
He own | boy drive | he + + + | a way
and he | own dog | ~~tear and~~ | … ~~tear~~ | ~~he skin~~

You love | as well | he who | look af | ter you | father | garden
who for | ever | bring you | box and | box of | + + + date
and ev | ery day | … [make | the ta | ble full]
You lift | you eye | to he | … you | go up | to he
"Garden | boy you | be strong | and beau | tiful
Hold out | you hand | and ~~touch~~ | ~~I sex~~!"
The gar | den boy | say to | you…
"What do | you want | + + + + + +?
Mother | if you | do not | cook + + + | I do | not eat
Shall I | [eat the | bread of] | ill will | … the | food of | evil?
Shall grass | + + + pro | tect me | against | the cold?"
You hear | he an | swer…
You strike | he and | turn he | in to | a fish
You set | he to | live… | in a | restaur | ant win | dow + + +
Where he | can move | + + + nei | ther in | or out

So you | will love | [DICTA | TOR in | turn] … | and he | will pay | for
   it'

When the | woman | sex god | hear this
she an | ger + + + | ~~she fly~~ | up to | the sky
and go | before | she fat | her the | sky god | AN + + +
Before | she moth | er the | wife of | the sky | god she | cry...
'Father | DICTA | TOR give | I the | bad mouth'

## Stone VI Cut iii

'DICTA | TOR speak | to I | of ill | will…
he speak | the bad | word a | bout I'

The sky | god AN | make of | he mouth | a shape | and move | he
    tongue
he say | to the | ~~woman~~ | sex god
'Hold on | + + + you | come on | to DIC | TATOR
like a | loving | machine | + + + + + +
and DIC | TATOR | point out | you do | evil
speak ill | of you | and send | you ~~word~~ | ~~bullet~~'

The wo | man sex | god make | of she | mouth a | shape and | move
    she | tongue + + +
Speak to | the sky | god AN | + + + + + +
'Father | give me | + + +  the | MAN COW | of the | sky he | will kill |
    DICTA | TOR in | ~~he home~~
make the |  MAN COW | feed on | the bone* (?) | of DIC | TATOR

*or 'body'

If you | do not | give me | the MAN | COW…
I will | open | … the | gate of | the un | der world
I will | fire up | the judge | of the | under | world + + +
I will | make the | dead rise | + + + and | they will | eat up | the ~~peo~~ |
    ~~ple of~~ | ~~the earth~~'

The sky | god AN | + + + move | he tongue | and speak | to the | woman
　| sex god
'If you | ask me | for the | ~~MAN COW~~
for sev | en year | in the | land of | big ci | ty of | the an | imal | noise
　no | thing will | grow but | ~~brush wood~~
Have you | store up | enough | + + + corn | for the | people?
Have you | enough | sugar | and tea?
Have you | enough | gas + + +?
Have you | enough | ~~grass~~ for | the an | imal?'

The wo | man sex | god move | she tongue | to speak
Say to | the sky | god she | father
'I have | enough | + + + corn | for the | people | in store
I have | enough | sugar | and tea | and gas
I have | ~~set grass~~ | ~~in store~~ | … for | the an | imal
If there | must be | seven | year + + + | of no | thing but | brush wood
I have | enough | corn + + + | for the | people
I have | enough | sugar | and tea
I have | enough | gas in | the dep | ot + + +
I have | set in | store grass | for all | the an | imal
… to | he… | ………… + + + + + +
……………… + + + + + + + + + + +
…… | ~~of the~~ | MAN COW'

Like a | lemon | the sky | god AN | + + + lis | ten to | the word | of the | woman | sex god

[He cre | ate for | she + + + | the MAN | COW of | the sky]

The wo | man sex | god + + + | drive [he | down to | the earth]

… [to | big ci | ty of | the an | imal | noise]…

… + + + + + + + + + + + + + + + + + + + + + + +

He go | down the | river | + + + + + + + + + + +

When the | MAN COW | of the | sky sneeze | a hole | open | up in | the earth

two hun | dred peo | ple of | big ci | ty of | the an | imal | noise ~~fall~~ | ~~in~~ ~~to~~ | ~~it~~…

## Stone VI Cut iv

…… | people

At the | second | sneeze a | hole op | en up | and two | hundred | people | fall in | to it

Two hun | dred peo | ple… | three hun | dred peo | ple…

Even | three hun | dred peo | ple of | big ci | ty of | the an | imal | noise fall | in to | it…

Even | four hun | dred peo | ple of | big ci | ty of | the an | imal | noise fall | in to | it…

At the | third sneeze | a…| hole op | en up | before | ~~WILDMAN~~

And all | the big | building | fall to | the ground

Even | the ap | artment | fall to | the ground

Even | the ar | ena | and the | audit | ori | um fall | to the | ground + + +

Even | the cha | pel and | the mo | tel fall | to the | ground + + +

+ + + + + + | the con | domin | ium | fall to | the ground

WILDMAN | fall on | the MAN | COW of | the sky

WILDMAN | jump up | and seize | the MAN | COW of | the sky | + + + take | hold of | he head | in a | strong head | lock + + +

The MAN | COW of | the sky | throw sand | in the | face of | WILD-MAN

He spit | in he | eye + + +

he show | he ~~bot~~ | ~~tom~~ to | WILDMAN


WILDMAN | make of | he mouth | a shape | and move | he tongue

he say | to DIC | TATOR

'Friend we | have be | come ~~great~~ | ……

How will | we + + + | over | throw he?

Friend I | know… | …………………

and strong | ... + + + + + + + + + + +
We will | destroy | ... + + + + + +
I... | + + + + + + + + + + + +
~~We must~~ | be strong | ... + + + + + +
We must | fill* (?)... | + + + + + + + + + + + +          *or 'kill'
... + + + + + + + + + + + + + + +
... and | stick* (?) he | behind* (?) | he* (?) neck'      *or 'kick'  *or 'in'
                                                                    *or 'the'

..........................................

WILDMAN | circle | about | ... he | run ~~round~~ | ~~the MAN~~ | ~~COW of~~ |
~~the sky~~
WILDMAN | hold he | ... and | [push he | face in | the dirt]

..........................................

# Stone VI Cut v

Then DIC | TATOR | like a | bad ~~moth~~ | ~~er~~ + + +
power | full... | ...... + + + + + + + + + + +
[strike] with | he knife | in the | + + + ~~neck~~ | [under | the ear]

After | they kill | the MAN | COW of | the sky | ... they | ~~cut out~~ | he
    heart
They lay | it be | fore the | sun god
They sit | down like | two blood | brother | on the | earth + + +

The wo | man sex | god go | up on | to the | wall of | big ci | ty of | the
    an | imal | noise...
In the | dress of | ~~one who~~ | ~~cry~~ she | speak the | bad word
'May ev | il come | to DIC | TATOR | ... who | make light | of I
who kill | the MAN | COW of | the sky!'

When WILD | MAN hear | the... | bad word | of the | woman | sex god
he tear | off the | leg* (?) of | the MAN | COW... | and throw | it in |
    she face                                     *or 'cut of meat'
'When I | can reach | you + + + | I will
tear off | + + + you | ~~leg too~~
I will | ~~push the~~ | ~~in side~~ | of the | MAN COW | in to | you face!'

The wo | man sex | god cry | out in | anger
she call | togeth | er the | holy | woman
the ~~top~~ | ~~shelf girl~~ | and the | hotel | girl + + + | the sex | worker
and ov | er the | leg of | the MAN | COW of | the sky | they start | ~~to~~
    ~~cry~~

DICTA | TOR call | togeth | er the | expert | of [the | city] | the art |
    man the | science | man the | business | man all
The young | expert | look at | the head | of the | MAN COW | of the |
    sky…
All + + + | over | it be | cover | with beau | tiful | ~~blue stone~~
+ + + thick | as two | finger | + + + side | by side
He car | ry + + + | [the head] | and hang | it in | the house | of he |
    father

They wash | they hand | + + + in | the great | river
They walk | hand in | hand as | they go

Each on | a horse | … they | ride through | the street | of big | city | of
    the | ani | mal noise
and the | people | of big | city | of the | ani | mal noise | gather | to
    look | on…
DICTA | TOR speak | to the | people | who ga | ther there
to the | woman | he say

## Stone VI Cut vi

'Who be | the jew | el of | all ~~bat~~ | ~~tle man~~?
Who a | mong all | people | have great | power?
DICTA | TOR be | the jew | el of | all bat | tle man
[WILDMAN] | among | all peo | ple have | great pow | er + + +
… they | be strong | + + + + + + | [toget | her] + + +
…… | the last | gift they | have not
…… | [sick]… | …………
In he | house + + + | DICTA | TOR hold | [a big | party]
The par | ty go | on all | night…
They make | a great | noise that | keep the | people | awake
The peo | ple cry | out in | they bed
[At last] | ~~they lie~~ | ~~down and~~ | go to | sleep on | the floor
among | the beer | can and | the wine | bottle | and the | whiskey
WILDMAN | when he | lie down | see a | dream…
WILDMAN | jump up | + + + to | set the | dream free
he op | en he | mouth to | speak and | throw up | instead | then say |
   to he | friend…

'Man… | why do | the great | god sit | ~~in court~~ | like bus | iness | men
   at | a board | meeting?'

## Stone VII Cut i

Then day | ~~light break~~ | ……

[And] WILD | MAN make | of he | mouth a | shape…

he say | to DIC | TATOR

'Listen | to the | dream I | dream in | the night

The sky | god | + + + the | war god | the ~~god~~ | ~~of know~~ | ~~ledge~~ and |
    the sun | god all | meet to | gether | in the | great court | of the |
    sky…

And the | sky god | AN + + + | say to | the war | god…

"Because | they kill | the MAN | COW of | the sky | + + + and | be-
    cause | they kill | TREEGUARD

the one* | who cut | down the | hard wood | tree on | the moun | tain
    side | must die"
                                            *DICTATOR

But the | war god | say + + + | "No it | is WILD | MAN that | [must
    die]

+ + + + + + | DICTA | TOR ~~can~~ | ~~not die~~"

Then the | sun god | of the | sky + + + | answer | the great | war god |
    he move | he tongue | and speak

"Listen | it is | I that | issue | the com | mand…

that they | kill the | MAN COW | of the | sky and | ~~TREEGUARD~~ |
    must now | blame less

WILDMAN | die?" But | the war | god turn

in an | ger to | the sun | god and | he say | "You say | this… | because |
    … like

a ~~friend~~ | you go | down to | talk to | WILDMAN | and DIC | TATOR |
    every | day…'"

WILDMAN | lie + + + | [sick] be | fore DIC | TATOR

Like a | patient | in a | hospit | al bed

As ~~tear~~ | ~~run down~~ | ~~he face~~ | [DICTA | TOR] say
'Brother | dear bro | ther! Must | I lose | you for | ever?' | + + +  And
'Must I | sit down | at ~~the~~ | ~~dark door~~
by the | shade [of | the dead]
and not | even | get you | a pres | cription
must I | sit down | at the | dark door
not ev | er [to | see] I | dear + + + | brother | [again]?'

## Stone VII Cut ii

WILDMAN | raise he | head and | open | he mouth | to speak | he say |
    to DIC | TATOR

'...... | in big | city | of the | ani | mal noise

[An old | friend can | say] a | strange thing | for sure

Why friend | do you | + + + say | such a | strange thing?'

As tear | run down | he face | DICTA | TOR say

'If the | + + + [dream | be] ~~sound~~ | ... + + + | the fear | be great

You arm | and leg | freeze + + + | like [one | who see | + + + death |
    pass by]

... if | the dream | be ~~sound~~ | + + + + + +

... for | the man | who live | it bring | great pain

the dream | will cause | the peo | ple... | who live | ... to | cry for |
    WILDMAN

... I | will pray | to the | great god | and god

I will | hunt out | and go | up to | the god | in the | sky + + + | AN + +
    +

...... | [to] the | ~~father~~ | ~~of all~~ | ~~the god~~

to the | war god | + + + and | argue | you case

I will | make for | you a | statue | of gold | with out | equal

.............................. + + + + + +

...... | do not | argue | + + + + + + | ... gold '

...........................................

The word | they speak | be not | the word | of an | ger + + +

They speak | ... He | do not | turn he | do not | [move]...

They look | ... He | do not | turn he | do not | move...

They ~~lis~~ | ~~ten~~... | He do | not turn | he do | not move

They breathe | ... He | do not | turn he | do not | move...

They cry | He do | not + + + | + + + + + + | + + + move

… + + + + + + + + + + + + + + + + + + + + + +

… + + + + + + + + + + + + + + +

… the | law of | the ~~sun~~ | ~~god~~…

…………………….

… + + + + + + + + +

…………………….

WILDMAN | shape he | mouth and | move he | tongue to | speak…
he say | to DIC | TATOR
'Get up | man + + +
Seek out | … the | [word of | the sun | god]…
+ + + find | the door | ……
~~in the~~ | ~~west~~… | …………
………………………….
+ + + + + + + + + + + +
………………,'


WILDMAN | … lift | [he eye]
in he | delir | ium | he speak | to the | door + + + | as to | a man
the great door that | they make | from the | wood of | the hard | wood
   tree
the great | door that | they bring | back to | big ci | ty of | the an | imal
   | noise + + +
'Door of | the wood* (?) | + + + emp | ty of | ~~knowledge~~

                                   *or 'door of wood'

the pow | er to | ear… | you do | not have
from a | great dis | tance I | wonder | at you | fine wood
even | before | I see | the ~~might~~ | ~~y~~ hard | wood tree | I see | fine wood |
   like you
No thing | [in all | the land] | can com | pare with | you wood

You be | one hun | dred foot | high you | be thir | ty… | …wide
you door | frame you | lock be | low and | above
Not once | door I | thought this | will come | to pass
… all | this + + + | ~~you beau~~ | ~~tiful~~ | [structure]
next time | I will | make you | with a | big… | knocker | + + + + + +
like on | the house | of a | doctor
Next time | I will | make you | a frame | of steel'

## Stone VII Cut iii

WILDMAN | move he | tongue to | speak…
… he | heart make | he bad | mouth CAT | CATCH…
'Make he | grow weak | + + + and | go in | to de | ficit
make the | road in | front of | he… | explode | [in he | face]…
make the | ani | mal run | from he
keep CAT | CATCH glass | ever | … half | empty'

He heart | make he | bad mouth | the top | shelf wo | man the | sex
   girl
'Listen | up… | woman | I can | see you | future
[a fu | ture] that | will have | no end | all bad
I will | put bad | word on | you… | maga | zine girl
At great | speed the | … stick | will strike | you + + +
Ever | will you | have ~~hun~~ | ~~ger~~…
and climb | the long | road to | the food | bank…
You will | love the | man who | ~~beat you~~
…………… | a slave | in the | black ec | onom | y…
………………… | live in | the dirt
………………… | hard ship
+ + + + + + + + + + + + | get hit
+ + + + + + + + + + + + + | get throw | out of | you house
……| the street | ~~will be~~ | you home
… [the | shade of | the wall] | will be | you place | of ~~rest~~
…… | you foot | in the | drain…
[the man | that drink | too much | will smash] | ~~you face~~
……………………………………………
+ + + + + + + + + + + + + + + + + + +

...........................
... + + + + + + + + + + + + + +
...... + + + + + +
.................
+ + + + + + + + + + + + + + + + +
..............................
because |  I..................
because | the spi | rit who | turn the | body | to stone | throw up | on
     WILD | MAN...'


The sun | god ear | the word | of WILD | MAN...
open | he mouth | to speak | and move | he tongue
and from | far off | from the | roof of | the... | sky he | call to | WILD-
     MAN
'Why do | you put | bad word | on the | love child | ... the | woman
who feed | you with | ~~the ho~~ | ~~ly~~... | ~~food~~ of | the sky
who give | you wine | to drink | that is | ~~the drink~~ | of the | rich...
who dress | you in | cloth of | ~~gold~~...
and give | you beau | tiful | DICTA | TOR as | a friend?


Listen | you friend |  DICTA | TOR do | he not | let you
lie down | in a | king size | bed...?
Do he | not let | you lie | down on | white sheet | and...
place you | on a | big... | seat by | he side* (?)?                    *or 'on the left'
The com | pany | chairman | he kiss | you foot


He will | make the | people | of ~~big~~ | ~~city~~ | ~~of the~~ | ~~ani~~ | ~~mal noise~~ | cry
     ov | er you | ... they | will cry | out to | remem | ber you
[he will | make the | woman] | ... the | whole ci | ty grow | sad o | ver
     you

And af | ter he | will co | ver he | body | with ~~long~~ | hair…
he will | put on | a ~~dog~~ | ~~skirt~~… | and walk | the wild'

WILDMAN | listen | to the | word of | the sun | god…
[and] the | anger | in he | heart grow | still…
… grow | cold…

## Stone VII Cut iv


'May [you | maga | zine girl] | return | home safe
May judge | diplo | mat and | ~~doctor~~ | love you
May no | one kick | a door | down be | cause of | you…
May no | old man | tear out | he hair | because | of you
May the | ~~one who~~ | ~~hold you~~ | bring you | treasure
[he will | give you] | jewel | ~~tele~~ | vision | and gold
May the | one who | sleep with | you pay | [you well]
… break | the bank
[May] you | go to | the par | ty of | the god | and god
May the | mother | of se | ven be | left to | cry be | cause of | you + + +'


… WILD | MAN [who] | be sick | in he | body
… lie | down all | by he | self…
[He go] | at night | [to tell] | ~~he friend~~ | he thought
'[Friend] a | dream come | to I | in the | dark + + +
The sky | ~~cry out~~ | earth mouth | off…
I stand | between | the two
[There be | a man] | he face | be black | as night
He face | be like | the face | of a | big cat
He foot | ~~print~~ be | the print | of a | big cat | he wing | be the | wing of
   | a great | bird…
He seize | a lock | of I | hair and | pull I | down + + +
… he | jump up
… he | push I | down…
… down | I go | ……
… I | body* (?) | ……                    *or 'head'
… + + + + + + + + +

... + + + + + + + + + + + + + +

.................. + + + + + +

... + + + + + + + + + + + + + + +

.................. + + + + + +.............

... + + +... + + + + + + + + +

... he | change I

... now | I arm | be like | the wing | of a | bird...

He seize | I and | lead I | down to | the house | of night | house of |
    shade...

the house | where he | who go | in do | not come | out a | gain...

the road | that if | you take | it you | do not | return

the house | that if | you live | there ~~there~~ | be no | elec | tricit | y...

the place | where they | live on | dirt and | the food | be poi | son...

where what | they wear | look like | ~~the wing~~ | of a | ~~bird~~...

and they | see no | light live | in the | dark...

all ov | er the | door and | on the | lock there | be dirt


In the | house of | ash where | I go

I see | the might | y one | fall down | in the | dirt + + +

I see | the might | y sol | dier one | who rule | over | the earth | in the
    | ~~old time~~

like a | god wait | at ta | ble with | cold meat

carry | bread and | fill the | cup with | water | from an | ani | mal skin


In the | house of | ash where | I go

there live | the ho | ly one | who bring | togeth | er god | and man |
    and the | one who | cry for | the dead

there live | the one | who wash | the foot | the wild | one who | sing
    the | spirit

there live | the ho | ly min | ister | of the | great god

there sit | the boy | that the | great bird | carry | off to | the sky | and
   there | sit the | cow god
There sit | the wo | man god | of the | under | world + + +
the book | woman | of the | under | world sit | before | she…
[she hold | a book] | and she | read out | ~~loud~~ from | it…
The wo | man god | of the | under | world lift | she head | and look | at
   I | – I…
"[Look] what | the cat | bring in | ……"'

## Stone VII Cut v
[WILDMAN dreams?]

[Badly flood damaged]


+ + + + + + + + + + +
+ + + + + +.....................
... + + + + + +.........
~~He~~... | + + + + + + + + + + +
...............................
+ + + + + + + + + + + + + + + + + + +
+ + + + + +
...... + + + + + +
+ + +...... + + + + + +...
... a | + + + + + +
+ + + + + +
+ + + + + +... + + +
... + + +
+ + + + + +
... [dream | of] + + +
+ + + + + + + + +...
+ + + + + +

## Stone VII Cut vi

WILDMAN | open | he mouth | and make | of he | tongue a | shape...
He say | to DIC | TATOR
'... show | WILDMAN | you wea | pon...
let WILD | MAN touch | the hard | steel...
... where | ever | I fly | + + + + + +
... where | ever | I look | + + + + + +
... who | ever | I ask | + + + + + +
I see | trouble | + + + + + +
Friend I | ... see | a dream | which be | a bad | dream...'

The day | he see | the ~~dream~~ | pass by
WILDMAN | lie still | ... like | a stat | ue... | a first | day a | second |
    day + + +
WILDMAN | + + + lie | ~~on the~~ | ~~bed~~... | under | the white | sheet...
three day | four day | WILDMAN | lie... | under | the white | sheet...
five six | seven | eight nine | [and ten | day]...
WILDMAN | lie | ...... | under | the sheet
ele | ven day | twelve day | thirteen | day...
WILDMAN | [lie down] | on the | bed like | a sick | ~~horse~~...
like a | horse that | will not | run an | other | race...

He call | DICTA | TOR...
'Man [some | god] put | a ve | to on | WILDMAN
I will | not die | like one | who fall | in bat | tle...
the  bat | tle bring | ...... | good luck | to the | one who | fall + + +
Man the | one who | [fall] in | battle | be world | famous | for fif | teen
    min | ute...

As for | WILDMAN | he will | die like | a dog

..................................
.......................................
...................................
...............................
...............................
... + + + + + + + +
+ + + + + + + + + + +
+ + + + + + + + + + +
+ + + + + +
+ + + + + + + + + + + + + + + + + + + + + +
+ + + + + + + + + + +
+ + + + +
+ + + + + '

## Stone VIII Cut i

When a | finger | of light | come…
DICTA | TOR op | en he | mouth and | speak…

'WILDMAN | …… | you moth | er be | a horse | ~~of the~~ | ~~valley~~
and… | you fat | her a | wild horse | of the | mountain
Ani | mal of | the wild | + + + ~~bring~~ | ~~you up~~
the crea | ture of | the wild | who have | a tail | behind
The path | that go | ~~up and~~ | down from | the fo | rest of | the hard |
    wood tree
cry for | you we | hear the | noise day | and night

The old | people | of big | city | of the | ani | mal noise | cry for |
    you…
They pray | for us | they wave | they fin | ger ~~in~~ | ~~the air~~
[as we | move up | the side] | of the | mountain* (?)

                                            *or 'corn mountain'

…… | as we | go up.

The grass | in the | field cry | for you | ~~like a~~ | mother
+ + + + + + + + + + + | the hard | wood tree.
………… | in the | forest | … the | ~~wild pig~~ | the wild | dog and | the
    big | cat cry | for you
The wild | pig the | wild dog | the wild | horse the | big cat
and the | wild cow | all the | ani | mal of | the for | est [cry | for you]
The wide | ~~river~~ | + + + where | we walk | down the | bank cry | for
    you

The pure | river | [where we | fill the | water | bag] ~~cry~~ | ~~for you~~
The + + + | people | of big | city | of the | ani | mal noise
where we | wonder | at [the | great wall] | where we | kill the | MAN
    COW | ~~of the~~ | ~~sky~~…
the peo | ple of | big ci | ty of | the an | imal | noise cry | for you
all who | praise you | name may | they cry | for you
the school | child the | mother | the bus | iness | man + + + | the ref |
    ugee
the peo | ple who | do not | yet praise | you name | may they | cry out |
    for you | too + + +


The wo | man who | put food | on you | plate may | she cry | for you
the one | who put | ~~butter~~ | before | you…
the one | who put | meat be | fore you
the one | who put | egg on | you plate | may she | cry for | you…
the one | who put | cheese be | fore you
the one | who put | maca | roni | on you | plate…
the one | who put | milk in | you tea
~~no you~~ | ~~do not~~ | ~~take milk~~ | ~~in you~~ | ~~tea~~ + + +
the one | who put | wine in | you mouth | … the | maga | zine girl
… [who] | cover | ~~you with~~ | ~~sweet oil~~ | she will | cry [for | you]…
[The house] | of the | man you | advise | about | a jew | el a | wife a |
    toothbrush
like bro | ther and | sister | they cry | for you.'

## Stone VIII Cut ii

'Listen | people | hear what | I say
To [you] | WILDMAN | I [use | to be] | a ~~moth~~ | ~~er~~ a | father
I will | cry out | for you | ~~in the~~ | ~~wild~~…
For WILD | MAN I | cry like | a wo | man once | happy | ~~now~~ sad
WILDMAN | + + + the | bullet | in the | gun the | bomb in | battle
the blade | in I | hand the | ammu | nition
I par | ty hat | + + + box | of ~~bright~~ | jewel

A great | evil | come and | steal he | a way

Friend you | hunt the | wild pig | the wild | horse of | the moun |
    tain…| wild cat | of the | valley
Once we | go to | gether | up in | to the | mountain
~~we bring~~ | ~~down~~ TREE | GUARD… | who live | in the | forest | of the |
    hard wood | tree + + +
we catch | the MAN | COW of | the sky | … and | kill it

Now sleep | take hold | of you
You grow | distant | + + + you | ~~can not~~ | ~~ear I~~'

WILDMAN | do not | lift he | head…
DICTA | TOR touch | he heart | it do | not beat

He ~~cov~~ | ~~er the~~ | ~~face of~~ | ~~he friend~~ | like the | face of | a girl | about |
    to ma | rry…

Like a | great bird | he cir | cle ov | er WILD | MAN + + +
Like a | wild cat | who lose | she child
Like a | mother | who lose | she child | to the | ocean
he walk | up and | down…
He ~~tear~~ | ~~out~~ he | hair and | it fall | to the | earth…
He tear | off and | throw down | he fine | coat in | the dirt

# Stone VIII Cut iii

'In a | place of | honour | I will | set you | up…
I will | put you | on the | [main stage]
I will | put you | out side | the bank
The great | people | of the | earth I | will… | order | to kiss | you foot

I will | have the | people | of big | city | of the | ani | mal noise | write
    songs | to re | member | you…
+ + + the | maga | zine girl | and the | ~~mili~~ | ~~tary~~ | man [will | cry] out

And af | ter I | [will co | ver I | body | with long | hair]…
I will | put on | + + + a | ~~dog skirt~~ | [and walk | the wild]'

When he | see a | finger | of light | come [DIC | TATOR]
He loose | he wide | collar | + + + + + +
……………………… stat | ue…
+ + + + + +…… + + + + + + + + + + +
+ + + + + +………… + + +…
+ + + + + +… + + +……… + + +
+ + +… + + + + + + + + + + +
………… + + + + + +…………
+ + + + + + + + + + + + + + + + +
…………………………… + + +
+ + + + + +………… + + + + +
+ + + + + + + + + + + + + + + + +
+ + + + + + + + + + + + + + + + +
+ + +…… + + +……
+ + + + + + + + + + +
*   *   *

# Stone VIII Cut iv

[The statue of WILDMAN described]


.................................................
.........................................
.......................................

+ + + + + + + + + + +
+ + + + + + + + + + +

.......................

+ + + + + + + + + + +
+ + + + +
*   *   *

... for | I friend | ..................
... a | blade... | of [stone] | + + + + + +
He see | the tool | + + + + + + + + + + + +
... stone | .................. | he shirt
... of | gold... | + + + + + +
..........................................

... he | heart be | not sick
+ + + + + + + + + + + +
... land | of the | sun god | ...... | out in | the hot | sun + + +
... ov | er the | world* (?)...                        *or 'word'
... he | will go | ......
... by | he side | + + + + + + | the blade
... he | [chest] be | of blue | stone...
... with | jewel | be it | cover | ...... | all ov | er + + +
... on | the main | stage + + + | + + + + + +

## Stone VIII Cut v

[DICTATOR makes an offering to the sun god]


+ + + + + + + + + + + + + + + + +

+ + + + + + + + + + +

.................. + + + + +

...... + + + + + +... + + +... + + +

+ + +...... + + +...... + + +

.................. + + + + +

...... + + + + + +... + + +... + + +

+ + +...... + + +...... + + +

... + + +... + + +... + + +

+ + + + + +... + + + + + + + + + +

+ + + + + + + + + + + + + + + + + + + + + +

... + + +... + + +... + + +

+ + + + + +...

+ + + + + +

+ + + + + +

* * *

... that | name we | ......

... judge | of the | under | world + + + | + + + + + +


DICTA | TOR ~~when~~ | ~~he hear~~ | ~~this~~...

he make | a pic | ture of | the ri | ver...

When a | ~~finger~~ | ~~of light~~ | come DIC | TATOR | make...

He put | toget | her a | large tab | le of | hard wood

he fill | a cup | of blue | stone with | milk...

+ + + he | paint it | and give | it to | the sun | god...

## Stone VIII Cut vi

[Content not known]

[Completely missing or damaged]

+ + + + + + + + + + + + + + + + +
+ + + + + + + + + + +
.................. + + + + +
...... + + + + + +... + + +... + + +
+ + +...... + + +...... + + +
.................. + + + + + +
...... + + + + + +... + + +... + + +
.................. + + + + + + + + + + + + + + + +
... + + +... + + +... + + + + + + + + + + + + + +
+ + + + + +... + + + + + + + + + + + + + + + + + + + + + + +
+ + +...... + + +...... + + + + + + + + + + + + + +
... + + +... + + +... + + +
+ + + + + +... + + + + + + + + + + +
+ + + + + + + + + + + + + + + + + + + + + + +
...... + + + + + +... + + +... + + +
+ + +...... + + +...... + + +
.................. + + + + + +
... + + +... + + +... + + +
+ + + + + +...
+ + + + +
+ + + + +
*   *   *

# Stone IX Cut i

DICTA | TOR cry | in pain | for he | + + + friend | WILDMAN
he walk | in the | hill and | hill… | lost… | in thought
'Hell!  Will | I too | not die | … ~~like~~ | WILDMAN?
Heavy | care fill | I stom | ach…
I fear | to die | to sleep | the sleep | that no | one a | wake from
I walk | over | the hill | and hill
I will | hit the | road I | will go | ~~at once~~
to the | house of | the ONE | WHO FIND | LIFE + + + | friend of | the
    god
… as | I come | near the | pass in | to the | mountain | at night
Big cat | I see | + + + and | I fill | with fear
I lift | I head | and I | pray to | the moon | god…
… I | look to | the + + + | moon god | and pray | for a | dream + + +
"…… | save DIC | TATOR!'"

…… | ~~though~~  he | lie down | [to sleep] | the dream* (?) | do not |
    come…                                *or 'picture'
… he | love life | like a | child of | the earth

In an | ger DIC | TATOR | take up | ~~he blade~~ | in he | hand…
he take | [the wea | pon] from | he side
[and] like | a bomb | [that ex | plode] + + + | he + + + | fall a | mong +
    + +
He strike | + + + ~~he~~ | ~~smash~~ + + +
+ + +  [en | joy] it
He ~~throw~~ | …… + + + + + + | a fit
he shout | …… + + + + + +

Smash + + + | ...... + + + + + +

He lift | ...... + + + + + + | the blade

.................. + + + + + +

...... + + + + + +... + + +... + + +

.................. + + + + + + + + + + + + + + + + + +

... + + +... + + +... + + + + + + + + + + +

+ + + + + +... + + + + + + + + + + + + + + + + + + + + + + + +

+ + +...... + + +...... + + + + + + + + + + + + + + +

... + + +... + + +... + + +

+ + + + + +... + + + + + + + + + + +

+ + + + + + + + + + + + + + + + + +

...... + + + + + +... + + +... + + +

+ + +...... + + +...... + + +

.................. + + + + + +

... + + +... + + +... + + +

+ + + + + +... + + +

+ + + + + + + + +

+ + + + + + + + +

*   *   *

## Stone IX Cut ii

[End damaged by building work]

[DICTA | TOR] go | up + + + | the moun | tain they | call Two | Moun-
tain
he come | near the | two top | [which one | should he | climb…?]
each day* (?) | the two | top guard | the home | of the | sun god

\* or 'night'

The top | and top | touch the | roof of | the sky
below | the foot | and foot | reach in | to the | ~~world of~~ | ~~the dead~~
Poison | six leg | people | guard the | door + + + | ~~through the~~ |
mountain
+ + + + + + | + + + + + + | they look | at you | you dead
the noise | of the | colon | y cov | er the | side of | the moun | tain…
When the | sun god | come and | go + + + | like sec | urit | y guard |
they watch | the door
that lead | ~~through the~~ | ~~mountain~~ | + + + where | the sun | god go |
down and | come up
When he | see the | poison | six leg | people | the face | of DIC | TA-
TOR | go dark | with fear
He ~~take~~ | ~~hold of~~ | ~~he self~~ | and he | go up | to they | [by a | path on |
the left]

The poi | son six | leg man | ~~call to~~ | he wo | man…
'The one | who come | here he | body | be like | a god'
The wo | man say | to the | poison | six leg | man…
'Two third | of he | be + + + | god and | one third | human'
The poi | son six | leg man | call out | to DIC | TATOR
he speak | to the | part god
['Why do | you tra | vel] + + + | so far?

[Why have | you] come | here be | fore us
[to this | place] that | is ~~hard~~ | ~~to tra~~ | ~~vel through~~?
Why do | you tr | avel | the hard | road like | a ref | ugee?
[I want | to know] | the rea | son that | you tra | vel here
[who] give | + + + per | mit + + +
+ + + spit | it out | + + + + + +'
+ + + + + + + + + + + + + + + + + +
+ + + + + + + + + + + + + +
+ + + + + + + + + + +
+ + + + + + + + + + + + + +
+ + + + + + + + + + + + + + + + + +
+ + + + + + + + + + + + + +
+ + + + + + + + + + + + + +
+ + + + + + + + + + +
+ + + + + + + + + + + + +
+ + + + + + + + + + + + + + + + +
+ + + + + +
+ + + + + + + +
*   *   *

# Stone IX Cut iii

\+ + + + + + + + + + + + + + + + +

\+ + + + + + + + + + + + + + + + +

'I have | come to | see the | ONE WHO | FIND LIFE | the fat | her of |
the tribe

who live | in the | compan | y [of | the god | and god | ~~and who~~ | ~~find
life~~]

[I want | to know] | the… | secret | of the | dead and | of life'


The poi | son six | leg man | shape he | mouth and | move he | tongue
to | speak + + +

he say | to DIC | TATOR

'Not ev | er be | fore have | a man | of the | earth come | to know | that
DIC | TATOR

No one | ever | travel | ~~the dark~~ | ~~path through~~ | ~~the moun~~ | ~~tain~~ + + +

for it | take twelve | horse one | truck to | reach the | centre

and thick | be the | dark + + + | ~~there be~~ | ~~no light~~

From the | time the | sun god | come out

To the | time the | sun god | go in

To the | ~~time the~~ | ~~sun god~~ | go in* (?)                           *or 'come out'

I be | the one | that make | the sun | god go | out…

I… | the one | that make | the sun | god go | in ag | ain + + +'

\+ + + + + + + + + + +

\+ + + + + + + + + + + + + + + + +

\+ + + + + + + + + + + + + + + + +

\+ + + + + + + + + + + +

\+ + + + + + + +

```
+ + + + +
+ + + + + + + +
+ + + + + + + +
+ + + + + + + +
+ + + + + + + +
*   *   *
```

## Stone IX Cut iv

'[Though I | face be | waste] by | hot and | [cold] + + +
Though I | body | be like | that of | a ref | ugee
Because | of the | pain [in | I side] | + + + + + +
I must | go  + + + | + + + + + + + + + + +
Now [op | en the | door through | the dark | mountain]'

The poi | son six | leg man | + + + [shape | he mouth | and move | he
   tongue | to speak]
to DIC | TATOR | [chief of | man] + + +
'Go DIC | TATOR | [+ + + go | in to]
the moun | tain + + + | ~~the two~~ | ~~top~~ + + +
Two Moun | tain home* (?) | [of the | sun god]                    *or 'hill'
Go in | peace + + +
[For you] | the door | ~~through the~~ | ~~mountain~~ | … [be | open]'

DICTA | TOR [lis | ten] to | the word | … [of | the poi | son six | leg
   man]
When he | hear this | he smile
[he take] | the road | of the | sun god

Like a | refu | gee + + + | + + + he | + + + tra | vel one | horse one |
   ~~truck~~ + + +
thick be | the dark | ~~there be~~ | ~~no light~~
he can | see not | back not | front not | about

Like a | refu | gee + + + | + + + he | + + + tra | vel two | horse one |
   truck + + +

## Stone IX Cut v

[thick be | the black | dark] there | ~~be no~~ | ~~light~~…
thick be | the air | he can | not breathe
he can | see ~~not~~ | ~~back not~~ | ~~front not~~ | [about]
+ + + + + + + + + + + + + + + + + + + + +

+ + + + + + + + + + + + + + + + + + + + +
+ + + + + + + + + + + + + + + + + + + + + + + +
+ + + + + + + + + + + + + + + + + + + + + + +

+ + + + + + + + + + + + + + + + + + + + +
+ + + + + + + + + + + + + + + + + + + + + + + +
+ + + + + + + + + + + + + + + + + + + + + +

+ + + + + + + + + + + + + + + + + + + + +
+ + + + + + + + + + + + + + + + + + + + + + + +
+ + + + + + + + + + + + + + + + + + + + + +

Like a | refu | gee + + + | he tra | vel four | horse ~~one~~ | ~~truck~~…
thick be | [the black | dark there | be no | light] + + +
thick be | the air | he can | not breathe
he can | see [not | back not | front not | about]

Like a | refu | gee + + + | [he tra | vel] five | horse ~~one~~ | ~~truck~~…
thick be | the [black | dark there | be no | light]…
he can | see not | back not | front not | about

+ + + + + + | + + + + + + | + + + + + + | he tra | vel six | horse one |
    truck + + +

thick be | the black | dark there | be no | light + + +
thick be | the air | he can | not breathe
he can | see not | ~~back not~~ | ~~front not~~ | ~~about~~

Like a | refu | gee + + + | he tra | vel sev | en horse | ~~one truck~~
thick be | the black | dark there | be no | light…
thick be | the air | he can | not breathe
he can | ~~see not~~ | ~~back not~~ | ~~front not~~ | ~~about~~

At eight | horse ~~one~~ | ~~truck~~… | he nu | clear | hot…
thick be | the black | dark there | be no | light…
he can | see not | back not | front not | about

At nine | horse ~~one~~ | ~~truck~~ + + + | the north | wind…
[bite in] | to he | face + + + | + + + + + +
thick be | the black | ~~dark there~~ | ~~be no~~ | ~~light~~…
~~he can~~ | ~~see not~~ | ~~back not~~ | ~~front not~~ | ~~about~~

At ten | horse ~~one~~ | ~~truck~~  + + + | + + + + + +
+ + + come | + + + + + + + + + + + + + + + + +
+ + + of | the horse | ~~one truck~~

After | elev | en horse | ~~one truck~~ | a blade | of light
After | twelve horse | ~~one truck~~ | the light | be strong
He see | the wood | of stone | and stone
the fruit | a red | jewel
[on] ~~branch~~ | and ~~branch~~ | good to | see…
the leaves | of blue | stone…
the fruit | beauti | ful to | the eye

# Stone IX Cut vi

[Damaged by flood]

[Description of the garden on the other side of the mountain]

..................................................
..................................................
....................................................
......................................................
.............................................
..................................................
.........................................
...................................

... app | le tree | ......

... tree | ~~bright with~~ | jewel | and jew | el...

[sea bright | stone and | stone]...

...

~~box~~...

ever | green...

..................................................
....................................................
..................................................
...............................................
..................................................

DICTA | TOR... | as he | go...

..................................................
..................................................
...............................................
............................
.............................................
.......................

\* \* \*

## Stone X Cut i

HOPE the | bar girl | from the | public | house at | the lip | of the | sea…
She mix | the drink | she hold | the glass
She op | en the | bottle | pour the | beer + + +
She wear | a pap | er  hat | + + + + + +
She smoke | she smile | + + + + + +

DICTA | TOR walk | to the | bar + + +
he wear | anim | al hide | ……
have the | [skin] of | a god | on he | body
pain in | the bread | basket
he look | like a | bad moth | er + + +
he face | ~~like that~~ | of a | man who | travel | far…

The bar | girl look | in the | distance
She say | to she | self + + +
'Where he | walk to | + + + + + + | this man
May be | this one | he out | to kill?'
When she | see him | come she | ~~bar the~~ | door…
She turn | the key | ~~she shut~~ | [the lock] | fast + + +

DICTA | TOR he | see it | all + + +
DICTA | TOR he | hear it | all + + +
he lift | he big | stick set | [he bo | dy be | fore the | door]…
DICTA | TOR move | he tongue | to speak | he say | to the | bar girl
'Bar girl | what do | you see | [that make | you shut | the lock]?

Why do | you turn | the key | why do | you bar | the door?
Speak or | I will | ~~smash down~~ | the door | and [break | the lock]'
+ + + + + + + + + + + + + + + +
+ + + + + + + + + + + + + + + + + +
… + + + + + + + + + + + +…
…………………… + + + + +
……………………………

The bar | girl she | speak to* (?) | DICTA | TOR…          *or 'point at'
'Why you | look like | you waste | a way | why you | face like | ruin?
+ + + ill | luck it | enter | you heart | enter | you eye
Pain be | in you | bread bas | ket…
You face | like that | of a | man who | travel | far…
You face | be weath | er by | hot and | cold + + +
You face | like that | of a | man who | run from | trouble
+ + + be | this why | you tra | vel the | wild af | ter a | bag of | wind…?'

DICTA | TOR op | en he | + + + mouth | to speak | to HOPE | the bar
    | girl…
'Bar girl | it be | not that | ill luck | enter | I heart
it be | not that | ill luck | enter I | ~~eye~~ + + +
it be | not the | pain in | I bread | basket
it be | not that | I run | from + + + | trouble
not for | that do | I tra | vel the | wild af | ter a | bag of | wind…
… but | because | of + + +
a friend | a broth | er who | hunt the | ~~wild horse~~ | the wild | cat of |
    the val | ley…
WILDMAN | + + + one | I love | who hunt | the wild | anim | al + + +
    | of the | valley

We ov | er pow | er all | climb the | mountain
catch and | kill the | MAN COW | of the | sky + + +
bring TREE | GUARD who | live in | the fo | rest  to | he end
bring cul | ture to | the wild
bring hard | wood to | the ci | ty + + +
in the | mountain | gate we | kill the | wild pig'

## Stone X Cut ii


'I friend | who I | love to | gether | we go | ~~through~~ great | hard ship
He pay | the debt | of man
WILDMAN | who I | love we | stick to | gether | through thick | and
    thin
~~He pay~~ | ~~the debt~~ | ~~of man~~
Six day | and sev | en night | I cry | over | he…
until | ~~a snake~~ | ~~fall out~~ | he nose
Then I | frighten
In fear | of death | I tra | vel the | wild… | the case | of I | friend lie |
    heavy | in I | heart + + +
I tra | vel a | long path | ~~through the~~ | ~~valley~~
How can | I keep | still?  How | … can | I find | peace + + +?
The friend | I love | he turn | to dust
WILDMAN | the friend | I love | + + + + + + | + + + dust
Will I | not lie | down like | he…
Will I | not pay | the debt | of man | too + + +?
to be | still for | ever | like stone?'


DICTA | TOR make | of he | mouth a | shape and | move he | tongue
    to | speak + + +
he say | to HOPE | the bar | girl…
'Now bar | girl… | which is | the way | to the | ONE WHO | FIND
    LIFE?
What be | the… | ~~land mark~~? | What be | the path?
If it | be poss | ible | I will | go ~~a~~ | ~~cross~~ the | sea…
If it | be not | possi | ble + + + | I will | travel | ~~across~~ | the wild'

The bar | girl make | of she | mouth a | shape | and speak | to he | to
    DIC | TATOR
'Forget | it… | DICTA | TOR no | one ev | er go | across | the sea
no one | in I | whole life | go a | cross the | sea…
No one | but the | sun god | go a | cross the | sea ex | cept for | he ~~no~~ |
    ~~one go~~ | ~~across~~
Full of | pain is | the way | … long | and hard | the road
and ev | en then | … the | water | of the | dead wait | for you
Even | if you | DICTA | TOR go | across | the sea
when you | arrive | at the | water | of the | dead + + + | what will | you
    do?
Down there | DICTA | TOR the | + + + boat | man of | the ONE |
    WHO FIND | LIFE live
The ~~stone~~ | statue | be with | he + + +
In the | ~~heart of~~ | the fo | rest he | lift up | the snake* (?) | that fly

*or 'tree'

Show he | you face
If it | be poss | ible | go ~~a~~ | ~~cross~~ with | he if | it be | not poss | ible |
    come back'


DICTA | TOR when | he hear | this + + +
+ + + he | + + + + + + | anger | + + + + + +
pull the | knife from | he bag
lift ~~the~~ | ~~blade~~ in | he hand
Quiet | he slip | along | the path | … and | go down | to the | forest
Like a | bomb + + + | he fall | ~~on they~~
in the | heart of | the fo | rest + + + | he make | battle
The boat | man see | the light | of the | knife…
hear the | blade + + +
Then DIC | TATOR | hit the | snake (?) that | fly on | the head

he hold | + + + the | wing tight | he [press | down on | the] ~~chest~~
and [he | smash] the | stone ~~stat~~ | ~~ue up~~
[he throw] | ~~the stone~~ | in the | water
he [throw] | the stone | [out of] | the boat
[the stone | statue] | with out | which no | one [go | across | the wa |
    ter of | the dead]
[no one | go a | cross] the | wide sea
on the | water | [of the | dead] + + +
+ + + + + + | to the | river
+ + + + + + | the boat
+ + + + + + + + + ~~on~~ | the bank
+ + + + + + + + + ~~the~~ | boat man
+ + + + + + | go down
+ + + you | + + + + + + | to he

# Stone X Cut iii

The boat | man make | of he | mouth a | shape and | move he |
    tongue…
he speak | to DIC | TATOR | he say
'Why you | ~~waste a~~ | ~~way~~… | why you | face like | ruin?
+ + + ill | luck en | ter you | heart… | enter | you eye
Pain fill | you bread | basket
You face | like that | ~~of a~~ | ~~man~~ who | travel | far…
You face | be weath | er + + + | by hot | and cold
You face | like that | of a | man who | run from | trouble
+ + + be | this why | you tra | vel the | wild… | ~~after~~ | ~~a bag~~ | of wind?'

DICTA | TOR make | of he | tongue a | shape and | move he | mouth
    to | … speak | he say | to the | boat man
'Boat man | it be | not that | ill luck | enter | I heart
it be | not that | ill luck | enter | I eye
it be | not ~~the~~ | ~~pain~~ in | I bread | basket
it be | not that | I run | from trou | ble + + +
not for | that do | I tra | vel the | wild af | ter a | bag of | wind… | ~~but~~
    [be | cause of]
a friend | a bro | ther who | hunt the | wild horse | + + + the | wild cat
    | of the | valley
WILDMAN | friend one | I love | who hunt | the wild | anim | al + + +
    | of the | valley
~~Toge~~ | ~~ther~~ we | over | power | all + + + | ~~toge~~ | ~~ther~~ we | climb the |
    mountain
catch and | kill the | + + + MAN | COW of | the sky
bring TREE | GUARD who | live in | the fo | rest ~~to~~ | ~~he end~~

bring cul | ture to | the wild
bring hard | wood to | the ci | ty + + +
in the | mountain | gate we | ~~kill the~~ | ~~wild pig~~
I friend | who I | love to | gether | we go | through great | hard ship
He pay | the debt | of man
Six day | and sev | en night | + + + I | cry ov | er he
until | a snake | ~~fall out~~ | ~~he nose~~
Then I | frighten
In fear | of death | ... I | travel | the wild
The case | of this | friend lie | heavy | in I | heart + + +
I tra | vel a | long path | ~~through the~~ | ~~valley~~
How can | I be | still? How | can I | live in | silence?
The friend | I love | turn to | dirt WILD | MAN the | friend I | love turn |
    to dirt
Will I | not lie | down + + + | like he
to be | still for | ever | like stone?'


The boat | man move | he tongue | and speak | he say | to ~~DIC~~ | ~~TATOR~~
'You heart | over | flow with | sad thought | you face | ~~look like~~ | ~~ruin~~
there be | pain in | you bread | basket
You face | be like | that of | a man | who tra | vel far
You face | be like | that of | a crim | inal | on the | run + + +
With the | hot and | cold + + + | you face | ~~weather~~
You tra | vel the | valley | after | a bag | of wind'


DICTA | TOR move | he mouth | and speak | to the | boat man | he say
'Enough | you know | now why | I waste | a way | like + + + | ruin
Why I | heart be | sad I | face ser | ious | like a | banker
You know | why pain | + + + fill | ~~I bread~~ | ~~basket~~
Now boat | man which | be the | way... | to the | ONE WHO | FIND LIFE?

What be | the land | mark ~~what~~ | ~~the sign~~ | to look | out for?
If it | be poss | ible | I will | go a | cross the | sea + + + | if not | I will |
   go back | in to | the wild'


The boat | man move | he tongue | and speak | to DIC | TATOR | he
   say
'What you | do back | there DIC | TATOR | ~~make the~~ | ~~way hard~~
~~You smash~~ | the stone | statue | + + + that | power* (?) | the boat
                                                        *or 'still'

~~and you~~ | ~~destroy~~ | the snake (?) | that fly
Now the | stone stat | ue live | just in | memory
you do | not find | the snake (?) | that fly | [in the | forest]
Lift up | the blade | in you | hand DIC | TATOR
go in | to the | forest | … [and | cut] some | ~~long stick~~ | ~~of nine~~ | ~~ty~~
   ~~foot~~
paint ~~thick~~ | ~~black paint~~ | on the | boss and | bring the | stick here'


DICTA | TOR when | he hear | + + + the | boat man
lift up | the blade | in he | hand + + +
he go | in to | the fo | rest [and | cut] some | ~~long stick~~ | ~~of nine~~ | ~~ty~~
   ~~foot~~
He paint | thick black | paint on | the boss | [and] bring | the long |
   stick back
DICTA | TOR and | the boat | man board | the boat
~~The boat~~ | ~~set sail~~ | they push | it through | the wave
In three | day they | travel | the dis | tance of | a month | and fif | teen
   day
The boat | man arr | ive at | the wa | ter of | the dead

# Stone X Cut iv

The boat | man op | en he | mouth and | move he | tongue to |
    speak…
he say | to DIC | TATOR
'Take care | man…
Do not | ~~touch the~~ | ~~water~~ | of the | dead with | you hand | ……
If you | do that | you ask | for trou | ble…
If you | do that | you have | bad debt | ……'

A sec | ond time | a third | time DIC | TATOR | ~~push the~~ | ~~boat~~ with |
    the long | stick…
Four five | six time | DICTA | TOR push | the boat | with ~~the~~ | ~~long~~
    ~~stick~~
Seven | eight nine | time DIC | TATOR | ~~push with~~ | ~~the~~ long | stick…
Ten el | even | twelve time | he push | + + + + + +
Thirteen | fourteen | fifteen | time + + + | DICTA | TOR push | with
    the | long stick
Sixteen | seven | teen eight | teen time | he push | with the | long
    stick
After | one hun | dred and | twenty | time DIC | TATOR | ~~wear all~~ | ~~the~~
    ~~long~~ | ~~stick out~~

The boat | man op | en he | mouth and | move he | tongue to |
    speak…
he say | to DIC | TATOR
'Now we | find trou | ble + + +
Look in | to the | water | and see | the face | and face | of the | dead + + +
who make | this jour | ney be | fore you'

Then DIC | TATOR | look in | to the | water | and he | see the | face
and | face of | the dead
He see | the face | of Ab | dul he | see the | face of | Abra | him + + +
He see | the face | of Mag | ga he | see the | face of | Bishu
He see | the face | of Bun | ta he | see the | face of | Michal
He see | the face | of Am | adou | + + + + + + | the face | of A | li + + +
He see | the face | of Im | ma he | see the | face of | Amel | ie + + +
He see | so ma | ny face | he start | to cry

The boat | man op | en he | mouth and | move he | tongue to |
speak…
he say | to DIC | TATOR
'Now is | the time | to pray'

When he | no lon | ger cry | DICTA | TOR sit | down in | the boat |
and pray
He say | a pray | er for | each face | he see | in the | water
One hour | he pray | two hour | he pray
Three hour | he pray | four hour | he pray
Then DIC | TATOR | stand up | + + + + ++

DICTA | TOR pull | ~~off the~~ | ~~coat~~ of | the [boat | man] so | that…
+ + + + + + + + + + + + + + + + + + + + + + + +
DICTA | TOR tear | off + + + | the shirt | of the | [boat man]
He make | the boat | man stand | with he | arm spread | out like | a
sail

The ONE | WHO FIND | LIFE look | on + + + | from the | distance
He make | he heart | hear ~~the~~ | ~~word he~~ | speak…
… hold | court with | he self

'Why be | the stone | statue | ~~all smash~~ | + + + + + +

and one | who be | not the | pilot | + + + + + + | why he | ride in | the
    boat?

The one | who come | be not | one of | I own | and...

I see | ~~but I~~ | ~~do not~~ | see... | ...............................

I see | but... | ...............................

I see | some thing | I do | not like | ......

... the | ani | mal... | ..................

...................................

...................................

... + + + + + + + +

+ + + + + + + + + + +

+ + + + + + + + + + +

+ + + + + +

+ + + + + + + + + + + + + + + + + + + + + + + +

+ + + + + + + + + + +

+ + + + + +

+ + + + + +'

## Stone X Cut v

DICTA | TOR make | of he | mouth a | shape and | move he | tongue
    to | speak + + +
He say | to the | ONE WHO | FIND LIFE
+ + + + + + + + + + + +
'...... | ani | mal + + +
+ + + + + + | not like
+ + + + + + | before | I + + +
...... | [one who] | travel | the wild
[hunt] the | wild cat | of the | valley
... kill | the... | + + + + + +
togeth | er we | climb the | mountain
hunt down | the MAN | COW of | the sky | + + + and | he kill
[bring TREE | GUARD to | he end] | who live | in the | hard wood |
    forest
[we en | ter the | door of | the moun | tain and | kill] the | big cat
[I friend | who I | love to | gether | we go | through great | hard ship]
[he pay | the debt | of man]
+ + + + + + | the end | that have | no cure
fill the | hole that | have no | bottom
feed on | the food | of the | dead...
[six day | and sev | en night] | I cry | for he
[I re | fuse to | bury | he] + + +
[until | a snake | drop out | he nose]
[I tra | vel the | wild] + + +
[I put | on an | imal | skin] and | set out | on a | long trip | ...
    through | the wild
+ + + + + + | I friend

he pay | the debt | of man | + + +

+ + + the | long road | + + + + + +

[How can | I live | in si | lence?] + + +

[I friend] | the one | I love | he turn | to dirt* (?) | WILDMAN | ......

*or 'bone'

Will I | not lie | down like | he + + + | and move | no more?'


DICTA | TOR make | of he | mouth a | shape and | move he | tongue to
   | speak...

He say | to he | to the | ONE WHO | FIND LIFE

'I say | to I | self "I | will go | to the | ONE WHO | FIND LIFE | the
   one | off the | map a | bout who | they tell | many | story"

I turn | and I | travel | ... ov | er all | the land

I cross | the high | mountain | + + + no | one ev | er cross

I tra | vel ov | er all | the sea

Sleep be | not a | friend to | I face

I go | with out | sleep and | wear I | self out | ... I | body | fill with | sad
   thought

Long be | fore I | arrive | at the | house of | the bar | girl... | I shirt |
   wear out

I kill | the big | cat the | wild dog | the wild | cow all | the wild | ani |
   mal of | the val | ley and | mountain

I eat | they bo | dy cov | er I | self with | they skin

She lock | the door | against | I + + + | + + + I | sleep in | the dirt

[I lie | down with | the an | imal | I touch ]

[I be] | the one | with out | luck the | one with | the ev | il eye | ......'


The ONE | WHO FIND | LIFE move | he tongue | to speak | and say |
   to he | to DIC | TATOR

'Why are | you sad | DICTA | TOR you

who be | part god | part man?
When you | father | and moth | er make | you in
the house | of the | god and | god they | ~~come to~~ | ~~gether~~
~~lie down~~ | ~~on the~~ | ~~bed~~ + + +
you fat | her be | foolish | you moth | er be | a god
They give | she to | he... | like but | ter for | old bread
like good | wine for | a hot | dog which | like...
+ + + + + + | quick like
and he | hold her | + + + ~~like~~ | ~~a horse~~
good wine | for a | [hot dog] | + + + + + +
... quick | like...
like... | + + + + + +
Why are | you sad | DICTA | TOR if | you have | the strength | of a |
    god + + +?
Why are | you sad | DICTA | TOR if | you must | pay the | debt of |
    man + + +?
as there | is no | future | for you | here  + + +
I have | no thing | to say | ......'

## Stone X Cut vi

+ + + + + + + + + + +
+ + + + + + + + + + +
a… | + + + + + + + + + + +
………………………………
+ + + + + + + + + + + + + + + + + +
+ + + + + + + + + + + + + + + + + + +
+ + + + + + + + + + +
+ + + + + +
+ + + + + + + +
… ~~an~~ | + + + + + +
+ + + + + +
+ + + + + +… + + +
… + + + + + + + + +
+ + + + + + + + + + + +
+ + +
+ + + + + + + + +…
+ + + + + +
…… | anger | ……
'Do we | build a | house to | last for | ever?
Do we | make a | deal to | last for | ever?
Do bro | ther and | brother | divide | proper | ty for | ever?
Does the | share rise | for ev | er + + +?
Does war | + + + + + + | + + + last | for ev | er…?
Does the | river | rise for | ever | to make | the land | … sea?
Does the | bird [leave] | the tree | ……
Does the | glass re | main full | + + + for | ever?
Does the | … ap | ple taste | ~~good for~~ | ever?

Does the | + + + girl | remain | beauti | ful for | ever?

Does mo | ney last | + + + for | ever?

Does a | toilet | roll + + + | + + + for | ever?

Does a | + + + new | car look | new for | ever?

Does a | + + + bank | lend for | ever?

Does the | + + + face | that look | at the | face + + + | of the | sun god

look at | the face | of the | sun god | for… | ever?

No thing | in the | world last | + + + for | ever

The one | who sleep | and the | one who | drink and | + + + the | dead
   they | be like | brother!

Do they | not all | look dead?

The man | in the | wild and | the great | business | man [be | they not
   | the same] | when they | arrive | + + + at | the end?

The chief | of pol | ice and | the ref | ugee | be they | not the | same
   when | they arr | ive at | the end?

The court | … of | the great | god and | god in | the sky

And the | one who | see the | future | fix the | end of | all thing

They give | life and | they take | it a | way…

The time | of life | be clear | to see | the time | of death | be sec | ret…'

## Stone XI Cut i

DICTA | TOR say | to the | ONE WHO | FIND LIFE | the one | off the |
    map + + +
'I look | at you | ONE WHO | FIND LIFE
You face | be no | differ | ent from | I face
You mouth | be no | differ | ent from | I mouth
You ear | be no | differ | ent from | I ear
You foot | be no | differ | ent from | I foot
You be | not diff | erent | from I | or I | from you
You heart | ~~burn for~~ | ~~battle~~
yet there | you sit | in com | fort you | lie on | you back
like a | man in | retire | ment + + +
or like | some one | on hol | iday
Tell DIC | TATOR | how you | go to | the ~~com~~ | ~~mittee~~ | ~~of the~~ | god... |
    and ask | for life'

The ONE | WHO FIND | LIFE op | en he | mouth and | make of | he
    tongue | a shape
he say | to DIC | TATOR
'I will | tell you | DICTA | TOR a | thing ~~that~~ | ~~no man~~ | ~~know~~...
tell you | ~~a see~~ | ~~ret~~ of | the god | and god

In a | foreign | city | you know | the place | I think
an old | city | once + + + | close to | the god | ~~and god~~
set on | the + + + | bank of | a wide | river
the great | god and | god tired | of the | noise and | the smoke
and the | end less | building | and beat | ing and | fighting | + + + + + +
thinking | that en | ough is | enough | decide | to cre | ate a | great wave

The great | mother | be there | and the | father | ~~of the~~ | ~~sky god~~ | AN
   + + +
and they | chief the | war god
the god | of ag | ricul | ture ~~guard~~ | of the | high seat | be there
and the | god who | inspect | the riv | er [and]
the god | of know | ledge he | of the | clear eye | be pres | ent too

[The god | of know | ledge] re | peat they | word to | a wall | of grass
"Grass wall! | Grass wall! | Wall! Wall!
Grass wall | … lis | ten! Lis | ten up!
Man of | the for | eign ci | ty…
ONE WHO | FIND LIFE
~~Tear down~~ | ~~this house~~ | and build | a boat
Give up | wealth and | choose life
~~Throw out~~ | ~~gold~~ and | hold on | to life
Load all | + + + life | on to | the boat
That you | will build
Measure | the meas | ure of | the boat
So that | it be | as wide | as long
Cover | it ~~with~~ | ~~a roof~~ | as the | sky be | cover | with cloud"

I hear | and un | derstand | I op | en I | mouth to | speak… | and say |
   to the | god of | knowledge
"Great god | what you | advise
I will | do in | + + + praise | ~~of you~~
But I | will have | to an | swer to | the peo | ple of | the ci | ty and | the
   old | man of | the cit | ty + + +"

The god | of know | ledge shape | he mouth | to speak
he say | to I | who serve
"You must | say this | to the | people
The war | rior | god he | hate I
I can | not stay | in the | city | or turn
I face | to the | land of | the war | rior | god…
I will | go down | ~~to the~~ | bottom | ~~to be~~ | with the | god of | knowl-
    edge
He will | make plen | ty rain | + + + down | on you
the beau | tiful | bird the | ~~rare fish~~
The + + + | land will | have a | mountain | of corn* (!)          *or 'ill luck'
At day | break he | will pour
+ + + rye | bread* (!) down | on you | a rain | of fish"'          *or 'dark'

## Stone XI Cut ii

'When a | ~~finger~~ | ~~of light~~ | come…
the peo | ple gath | er…
……………………………
……………………………
… the | young man | who run | with the | wind…
… the | young wo | man who | run with | the wind
to the | house of | … grass
the child | carry | + + + ~~thick~~ | ~~black paint~~
the strong | bring what | ever | else we | need…

After | five day | I make | a plan
The whole | floor ar | ea | be fif | ty thou | sand square | foot the |
    height of | each wall | be one | hundred | and ~~eight~~ | ~~y foot~~
the top | be one | hundred | and eight | y foot | square on | each side
I de | sign it | all + + + | ~~spread out~~ | ~~the plan~~
I give | it six | + + + + + + | floor…
~~and so~~ | ~~divide~~ | ~~it in~~ | ~~seven~~ | ~~level~~
The in | side I | ~~divide~~ | in nine | + + + + + + | + + + ar | ea
I drive | strong wed | ges + + + | + + + cut | from wood | in to | any |
    hole in | the wall
I count | out the | ~~long stick~~ | … and | bring in | all that | we want
On the | back end | I use | up ten | thousand | can of | black paint
the same | amount | I put | on the | ~~in side~~
In a | big bas | ket the | young boy | bring on | three hun | dred weight |
    of oil
as well | as a | hundred | weight of | oil to | serve for | water | proofing

and two | hundred | weight of | ~~oil that~~ | ~~I give~~ | to the | boat man | …
   for | the store

I kill | ten man | cow for | the peo | ple…
and kill | a new | pig ev | ery day
Drink and | oil + + + | and wine
I give | to the | work man | and work | man to | swallow | as if | it be |
   river | water
… so | that they | ~~party~~ | ~~like at~~ | New Year
I op | en the | ~~body~~ | ~~butter~~ | and spread | it on | I hand
After | seven | day the | boat be | ready
The hard | work be | gin + + + | when we | set sail
The peo | ple push | + + + + + + | the boat | hard ~~a~~ | ~~bove and~~ | ~~below~~
until | two third | + + + of | the struc | ture ~~en~~ | ~~ter the~~ | ~~water~~
All I | possess | I load | in to | the boat
All I | have in | the bank | I take | out + + +
all I | have of | silver | + + + ~~I~~ | ~~load on~~
all I | have of | gold ~~I~~ | ~~load on~~
all I | jewel | I load | on…
I load | on soup | I load | on stew
I load | on oats | and chill | i and | cabbage
I load | on grape | fruit I | load on | honey
and lob | ster and | beer and | pasta
I load | on cheese | I load | on tun | a + + +
+ + + jam | and broc | coli | and cake
I load | on sau | erkraut | + + + + + + | + + + bran
I load | on pine | apple | and cat | fish and | pumpkin
all I | famil | y I | make en | ter the | boat…
The an | imal | of the | field and | the wild | ani | mal of | the fo |
   rest… | and the | child of | all the | boat man | I drive | on board

The war | god set | the time
"In the | morning | he will | send down | a ~~rain~~ | ~~of~~ + + + | ~~rye bread~~ (!)
At night | he will | send down | a rain | of fish
enter | the boat | and ~~close~~ | ~~the door~~"

The hour | come near
"In the | morning | he will | send down | a rain | of + + + | rye bread (!)
At night | he will | send down | a rain | of corn (!)"
I see | day come | on…
To look | on that | day fill | I with | terror
I go | in to | the boat | and ~~close~~ | ~~the door~~
To the | one who | paint the | boat… | I give
~~the house~~ | ~~and all~~ | ~~that be~~ | ~~in it~~'

# Stone XI Cut iii

'When a | ~~finger~~ | ~~of light~~ | begin | to ap | pear…
a ~~black~~ | ~~cloud~~ + + + | rise up | from the | distance
From ~~with~~ | ~~in it~~ | the storm | god cry | out loud
The god | of ru | in and | the god | of con | trol run | before | it…
they move | like an | ~~enem~~ | ~~y hel~~ | ~~icop~~ | ~~ter~~ + + + | over | the moun |
    tain and | the land
The god | of the | under | world break | he door | frame + + +
The son | of the | war god | come + + + | he make | the riv | er ~~burst~~ |
    ~~the bank~~
The man | y judge | of the | god lift | up and | shine they | light + + +
the land | shine bright | + + + un | der the | radi | ation
The can | cer of | the storm | god ~~eat~~ | ~~up the~~ | ~~sky~~…
turn all | that be | light ~~to~~ | ~~dark~~ + + +
The wide | land smash | like a | wine glass

For one | whole day | the south | wind blow
it tear | up the | tree and | the buil | ding + + +
it throw | the car | up in | the air
it throw | the con | domin | ium | to the | ground + + +
even | the cha | pel and | the mo | tel fall | to the | ground + + +
it gath | er speed | and ex | plode + + + | on the | mountain
lay the | tree flat | like grass
Like a | nucle | ar win | ter + + + | ~~it stretch~~ | ~~over~~ | ~~ever~~ | ~~y thing~~
All go | dark + + +
brother | ~~can not~~ | ~~see~~ + + + | brother
from the | sky no | one can | see the | people | at all
the big | water | frighten | even | the god

they run | off back | to the | home of | the sky | god AN
Each god | ~~like a~~ | ~~dog~~ in | a bas | ket lie | out side | [he door]

The wo | man sex | god cry | out like | a wo | man in | labour
in she | sweet voice | she cry | out…
"All of | the old | world ~~turn~~ | ~~to dirt~~
since I | speak ev | il in | the court | of the | god…
How can | I speak | evil | in the | court of | the god?
How can | I cry | out for | battle | + + + for | ~~the end~~ | ~~of I~~ | ~~people~~?
I own | self give | birth + + + | to I | people!
[Now] like | the off | spring of | fish they | will fill | the sea!"

Even | the man | y judge | of the | god cry | with she
the god | and god | in shame | … sit | and cry
all to | gether | …… | ~~they lip~~ | ~~be tight~~

Six day | and sev | en night
the wind | cry like | a wo | man in | labour
… and | the storm | tear through | the land
After | seven | day… | the storm | ~~break off~~ | from the | battle
all go | still as | the grave
The sea | grow qui | et the | storm still | the big | water | stop…
I look | out at | the day | and all | be still
All the | ~~people~~ | ~~lie dead~~ | … in | the dirt* (?)                    *or 'water'
The ground | be like | ~~a great~~ | ~~flat roof~~
I op | en the | window | and light | fall on | I face
I sit | down and | cry…
The tear | flow down | I face

I look | out for | land ~~at~~ | ~~the edge~~ | ~~of the~~ | ~~sea~~…
and af | ter I | look twelve | time I | see an | island
The boat | stand still | on the | mountain
The moun | tain ~~seize~~ | ~~the boat~~ | it can | not rise
A first | day… | a sec | ond day | the boat | stick on | the moun | tain +
    + +
Three day | and four | day the | boat stick | on the | mountain
Five six | day the | boat stick | on the | mountain
Day sev | en when | it arr | ive…'

## Stone XI Cut iv

'I send | out a | white bird | … ~~off~~ | ~~it fly~~
The white | bird go | out and | come back
It can | see ~~no~~ | ~~place to~~ | ~~rest~~ + + + | so it | turn back

I send | out a | swallow | …off | it fly
The swal | low go | out ~~and~~ | ~~come back~~
It can | ~~see no~~ | ~~place to~~ | ~~rest~~ + + + | so it | turn back

I send | out a | black bird | …off | it fly
The black | bird go | out and | see that | the wa | ter go | ~~down~~…
it fly | about | eat and | circle | but it | ~~do not~~ | ~~come back~~

I send | they out | to the | four wind | … and | make a | sacri | fice to |
    the god | and god
I put | out a | gift of | drink in | the ho | ~~ly place~~ | on the | mountain
seven | and sev | en ho | ly cup | ~~I set~~ | ~~down~~ + + +
Round the | holy | cup… | I pour | flower | water
The ~~god~~ | ~~and god~~ | smell the | water
the god | and god | smell the | sweet wa | ter…
and they | gather | ~~like fly~~ | ~~and fly~~ | + + + round | the sac | rifice

From far | off the | woman | sex god | come down | to earth
[From the | dead bo | dy ov | er the | earth] she | lift up | the bright |
    fly jew | el which | the sky | god cre | ate for | the ~~love~~ | ~~hour~~…
"God and | god by | the pow | er of | the blue | stone round | I neck | I
    will | not for | get this
This ev | il day | I will | ~~remem~~ | ~~ber for~~ | ~~ever~~

Gather | round the | sacri | fice…

But the | war god | must not | come near | the sac | rifice

for with | out the | agree | ment of | the [com | mittee | of the | god]
    he | bring down | the ~~great~~ | ~~water~~

… and | I peo | ple he | single | out for | death + + +"


As soon | as the | ~~war god~~ | arrive

the hot | head see | the boat

He fill | up with | ~~the an~~ | ~~ger of~~ | ~~seven~~ | ~~god~~…

"Be life | ~~that breathe~~ | still here? | I bring | the great | water | + + + ~~to~~
    | ~~destroy~~ | ~~all life~~!"


The god | of ag | ricul | ture ~~shape~~ | ~~he mouth~~ | ~~to speak~~ | and move |
    he tongue

he say | to the | war god

"Who but | the god | of know | ledge can | create | a thing* (?)?

*or 'plan'

The god | of know | ledge know | the word* (?)"      *or 'message'


The god | of know | ledge shape | he mouth | to speak | and move | he
    tongue

he say | to the | war god

"You wise | one a | mong the | god + + + | ~~war god~~

how is | it that | with out | any | debate | ~~you send~~ | ~~the great~~ | ~~water~~?

Punish | the one | who do | the crime | punish | ~~the one~~ | ~~who do~~ |
    ~~evil~~

Put he | ~~in pri~~ | ~~son~~ so | he be | not free | + + + tor | ture he | to make
    | he speak

Before | you cre | ate the | great wa | ter… | make the | big cat | rise up
| and at | tack the | people

Before | you cre | ate ~~the~~ | ~~great wa~~ | ~~ter~~ make | the wild | dog + + + |
rise up | and drive | the peo | ple back

Before | you cre | ate the | great wa | ter make | the corn | fail ~~to~~ |
~~bring the~~ | ~~land low~~

Before | you cre | ate the | great wa | ter make | disease | rise up | and
strike | the peo | ple down


No way | do I | grass the | ~~secret~~ | of the | great god
[The ONE | WHO FIND | LIFE] the | over | wise… | ~~see a~~ | ~~dream~~
where | he hear | the sec | ret of | the god"


Think a | bout what | [the god | of know | ledge] + + + | say [DIC |
TATOR]


The war | god come | up to | the boat
He take | I hand | ~~and lift~~ | ~~I up~~
and he | raise I | wife up | … and | make she | sit at | I side
Then he | ~~touch I~~ | ~~head~~ + + + | and I | wife head | and speak | before |
the god | and god


"Before | this the | ONE WHO | FIND LIFE | be just | a man
Now the | ONE WHO | FIND LIFE | and he | wife be | change… |
now he | be ~~like~~ | ~~a god~~
From now | the ONE | WHO FIND | LIFE will | live far | off + + + | at
the | ~~secret~~ | ~~birth place~~ | ~~of the~~ | ~~river~~"

Then they | take I | far off | to live | at the | secret | ~~birth place~~ | of the | river

    river

like a | man in | retire | ment + + +


Now DIC | TATOR | who will | gather | the god | and god | to bring | to you

    you

so that | you can | find the | + + + life | that you | look for?


You must | take a | test! Do | not sleep | for… | six day | ~~and sev~~ | ~~en night~~'

    ~~night~~'


Even | as he | sit there | + + + be | fore the | ~~ONE WHO~~ | ~~FIND LIFE~~

sleep like | a wet | mist + + + | blow ov | er he


The ONE | WHO FIND | LIFE say | to he | wife…

'Look at | this great | + + + man | who ask | for life!

Sleep blow | over | he… | like a | wet mist!'


He wife | answer | the ONE | WHO FIND | LIFE… | the far | off one

'Touch the | man so | that he | awake

He will | take the | road and | ~~go back~~ | ~~in peace~~

He will | go out | ~~through the~~ | ~~gate~~ + + + | back to | he land'


The ONE | WHO FIND | LIFE say | to he | wife…

'A man | who be | trouble | + + + will | ~~give you~~ | trouble

Come make | bread for | he place | it near | he by | he head | each day

and each | day he | sleep + + + | ~~mark on~~ | ~~the wall~~'


She make | bread for | he + + + | and set | it by | he head

and each | day he | sleep she | ~~mark~~ on | the wall

The bread | of the | first day | go hard | like a | rock + + +
the bread | of the | ~~second~~ | + + + be | like an | old shoe
the third | be all | dark + + + | the fourth | turn white
the fifth | have grey | on it | + + + the | sixth give | off ~~a~~ | ~~bad smell~~
the sev | enth
                Of | a sud | den as | the ONE | WHO FIND | LIFE
       touch | ~~the man~~ | he jump up | up + + +

## Stone XI Cut v

DICTA | TOR op | en he | mouth to | speak and | move he | tongue…
he say | to the | ONE WHO | FIND LIFE | the one | off the | map + + +
'As soon | as I | begin | to sleep
right a | way you | ~~touch I~~ | and I | awake'

The ONE | WHO FIND | LIFE make | of he | mouth a | shape and |
    move he | tongue to | speak + + +
he say | to he | to DIC | TATOR
'Come on | DICTA | TOR… | look at | the bread
I will | show you | how man | y day | you sleep
The bread | of the | first day | be ~~hard~~ | ~~as rock~~
the sec | ond be | like an | old shoe | + + + the | third be | ~~all dark~~ |
    the fourth | turn white
~~the fifth~~ | ~~have grey~~ | ~~on it~~ | … the | sixth give | off a | bad smell
the sev | enth + + + | + + + all | of a | sudden | as I | touch you | you
    jump | up + + +'

DICTA | TOR op | en he | mouth to | speak and | move he | tongue…
he say | to he | to the | ONE WHO | FIND LIFE | … the | one off | the
    map
'What should | I do | ONE WHO | FIND LIFE? | ~~Where should~~ | ~~I go~~?
A dead | man ~~steal~~ | ~~in to~~ | ~~I skin~~
The dead | live in | the house | where I | bed be
and where | ever | I set | foot + + + | ~~there be~~ | ~~the dead~~'

The ONE | WHO FIND | LIFE op | en he | mouth and | move he | tongue…

he say | to the | boat man

'Boat man | [from now | on] ~~the~~ | ~~port will~~ | ~~refuse~~ | ~~you~~… | …the | boat trip | will be | a thing | you hate

For a | long time | you have | come to | this port | [from now | on] the | port will | ~~be shut~~ | to you

Thick hair | cover | the bo | dy of | the man | you bring | here…

Ani | mal hide | cover | he ~~beau~~ | ~~tiful~~ | ~~skin~~…

Lead he | to the | sea + + + | where he | can wash | boat man

Make he | ~~wash off~~ | ~~the dirt~~ | from he | body | hair in | water | and be | come pure

Make he | throw the | ani | mal hide | in to | the sea | and let | the good | of he | body | shine out

~~Tie back~~ | ~~the~~ + + + | ~~hair on~~ | ~~he head~~ | ~~again~~

Have he | put on | cloth… | the cloth | of life

so that | he may | return | to big | city | of the | ani | mal noise

so that | he may | now go | ~~the rest~~ | ~~of the~~ | ~~way~~ down | the road | of life

Have he | dress like | an old | man of | the ci | ty court | … and | look ev | er new'


The boat | man take | [charge] of | he + + + | and bring | he to | the sea | where he | can wash

He clean | ~~the dirt~~ | ~~from he~~ | ~~body~~ | ~~hair~~ in | the wa | ter + + + | and make | he pure

He throw | the an | imal | hide in | to the | sea…

the good | of he | body | shine out

~~He tie~~ | ~~back the~~ | ~~hair on~~ | ~~he head~~ | ~~again~~

and put | cloth on | he… | the cloth | of life
so that | he can | go back | to big | city | of the | ani | mal noise
so that | he may | go ~~the~~ | ~~rest of~~ | ~~the way~~ | down the | road… | of life
He dress | like an | old man | ~~of the~~ | ~~city~~ | ~~court~~ and | look ev | er new

DICTA | TOR and | the boat | man get | on to | the boat
They lift | the boat | ~~in to~~ | ~~the wave~~ | and go

## Stone XI Cut vi

Then he | wife op | en she | mouth and | move she | tongue to |
    speak…
she say | to he | to the | ONE WHO | FIND LIFE | … the | far off
'DICTA | TOR come | here… | ~~he bat~~ | ~~tle~~ and | he bend* (?)

                                      *or 'burn'

What do | you give | he when | he re | turn ~~home~~?'

At that | DICTA | TOR lift | ~~he long~~ | ~~stick~~ + + +
and bring | ~~the boat~~ | close to | the land | again

The ONE | WHO FIND | LIFE make | of he | mouth a | shape and |
    speak…
he say | to he | to DIC | TATOR
'DICTA | TOR you | come here | you bat | tle and | you bend (?)
What can | I give | you as | you re | turn home?
I will | show you | ~~a see~~ | ~~ret thing~~ | DICTA | TOR…
I will | tell you | ~~a see~~ | ~~ret of~~ | ~~the god~~
I know | a plant | the ~~root~~ | ~~go deep~~ | like a | box tree
the leaf | ~~will cut~~ | ~~you like~~ | ~~a knife~~
If you | get hold | of that | plant… | you will | live for | ever
and if | you make | a cream | out of | that plant | you will | be a | rich
    man'

DICTA | TOR when | he hear | this he | open | the hold
He ~~tie~~ | ~~a stone~~ | ~~block~~ to | he foot
~~it pull~~ | ~~he down~~ | ~~to the~~ | ~~bottom~~ | + + + and | he see | the plant
He seize | the plant | + + + though | it cut | in to | he hand

he cut | the stone | block from | he foot
the sea | throw he | up on | to the | land like | a cork

DICTA | TOR op | en he | mouth and | make of | he tongue | a shape
he say | to the | boat man
'Boat man | this plant | be like | a door
by which | a man | can get | life…
I will | carry | it to | big ci | ty of | the an | imal | noise… | I will | give
   it | to the | old to | eat they | will div | ide the | plant out
The name | of the | plant will | be… | THE OLD | MAN WILL | BE
   YOUNG | AGAIN
I too | will eat | it and | I will | be a | young man | again
I will | make a | cream out | of it
The name | of the | brand will | be FOR | EVER'

At twen | ty horse | + + + they | [break off | for a] | + + + bite | to eat
sit tight | in the | boat + + + | + + + + + +
At thir | ty horse | they take | a look | at the | + + + map
which blow | about in | the + + + | + + + wind
+ + + + + + | but they | are still | + + + + + + | off the | map + + +
At for | ty horse | they see | land + + + | in the | distance
At fif | ty horse | they [break off | for a] | + + + smoke
At six | ty horse | they get | ready | for the | night …
DICTA | TOR see | a lake | of cool | water
He go | down to | it + + + | and wash | in the | water
A snake | smell the | fresh smell | of the | plant …
It come | up through | the wa | ter and | carry | the plant | off …
As it | turn it | throw off | it skin

That day | DICTA | TOR sit | down and | cry + + +
Over | he face | + + + the | tear flow
He take | the hand | of the | boat man
'For who | + + + boat | man do | I bend | I arm?
For what | be the | blood ~~of~~ | ~~I heart~~ | all dry?
I do | not win | any | good for | I self
it be | the snake | that win | ~~good luck~~
Now the | river | will car | ry it | off...
When I | see the | + + + lake | of cool | water
I make | a big | mistake
come we | must go
~~and leave~~ | ~~the boat~~ | here'

                                  At | twenty | horse they | ~~break off~~ | for a |
    + + + smoke
At thir | ty horse | they take | a look | at the | road map
At for | ty horse | they + + + | get rea | dy for | the night
At fif | ty horse | they walk | all day | + + + get | sun burn
At six | ty horse | they break | off for | a can | of beer
The dis | tance of | two month | and ten | and four | day they | travel |
    in five | + + + day
They arr | ive at | big ci | ty of | the an | imal | noise...

DICTA | TOR make | of he | mouth a | shape and | move he | tongue
    to | speak...
he say | to he | to the | boat man
'Go up | boat man | ~~on to~~ | ~~the wall~~ | of big | city | of the | ani | mal
    noise
Exam | ine + + + | the base | look at | the per | fect brick | work
    straight | and true

Clock that | even | the cen | tre is | of good | fire brick
As for | the base | be it | not set | + + + down | by a | wise man?

In [big | city | of the | ani | mal noise] | house of | the wo | man sex |
    god + + + | one part | be ci | ty one | part fruit | tree one | part mine
Three part | with the | mine make | up big | city | of the | ani | mal
    noise'

## Stone XII Cut i

DICTA | TOR make | of he | mouth a | shape and | move he | tongue
   to | speak…
he say | to he | to + + + | WILDMAN
'I want | + + + the | ~~ball and~~ | ~~stick~~ back
safe at | the house | of the | one who | model | in wood!
safe + + + | with he | wife + + + | who be | like a | mother | to I!'

WILDMAN | move he | tongue to | speak he | say to | DICTA | TOR
   + + +
'Man… | why be | ~~you heart~~ | ~~heavy~~?
So what | if you | lose the | ball and | stick…?
I will | bring up | the ball | from the | under | world… | from the |
   land of | the dead
I will | bring up | the stick | ~~from the~~ | ~~dark mouth~~ | of the | under |
   world + + +'

DICTA | TOR make | of he | mouth a | shape and | move he | tongue
   to | speak + + +
he say | + + + ~~to~~ | ~~WILDMAN~~
'If you | go down | + + + to | where the | earth cry
remem | ber + + + | the ~~see~~ | ~~ret~~ I | tell you
Listen | … to | what I | advise'

DICTA | TOR make | of he | tongue a | shape and | speak + + +
he say | to he | + + + to | WILDMAN
'Any | one who | go down | in to | ~~the un~~ | ~~der world~~
must re | member | what I | say + + +

Do not | ~~put on~~ | ~~a clean~~ | ~~shirt~~…
It will | + + + mark | you out | as + + + | from up | here + + +
Do not | put sweet | oil from | a bot | tle on | you skin* (?)    *or 'hair'
They will | gather | and set | tle all | round you | like fly
Do not | hit out | with you | ~~sharp stick~~ | + + + in | the un | der world
The one | hit by | the stick | will turn | on you
Do not | carry | a cell | phone in | you hand
The dead | + + + will | give you | the ev | il word
Do not | put a | shoe on | ~~you foot~~
Do not | shout in | the place | or cry | out + + +
Kiss not | ~~the wife~~ | ~~you love~~
or beat | the wife | you hate
Kiss not | the child | you love
or beat | ~~the child~~ | ~~you hate~~
or you | will find | trouble

The voice | of the | dead ~~will~~ | ~~sing out~~
*She who | sleep she | who sleep | mother | of birth | and of | the dead | who sleep*
*No cloth | cover | she + + + | clean neck*
*She chest | which be | like a | cold stone | + + + do | not feed | the child'*

## Stone XII Cut ii

DICTA | TOR warn | he but | WILDMAN | ~~do not~~ | ~~listen~~
the word | go in | one ear | and out | the oth | er + + +
He put | on a | clean shirt
It mark | he out | as + + + | from up | here + + +
He put | sweet oil | + + + from | a bot | tle on | he skin (?)
When they | smell it | + + + they | ~~gather~~ | ~~round he~~ | like fly
In the | under | world ~~he~~ | hit out | with he | ~~sharp stick~~
and the | dead peo | ple ~~hit~~ | ~~by the~~ | ~~stick~~ turn | on he
He car | ry a | … cell | phone in | he hand
put new | shoe ~~on~~ | ~~he foot~~
He cause | a ri | ot in | the un | der world
~~He kiss~~ | the wife | he love
and beat | the wife | he hate
~~he kiss~~ | the child | he love
and beat | the child | he hate

The voice | of all | the dead | sing out | toget | her + + +
*She who | sleep she | who sleep | mother | of birth | and of | the dead | who sleep*
*No + + + | cloth cov | er she | clean neck*
*She chest | which be | like a | cold stone | + + + do | not feed | the child*

She do | not per | mit WILD | MAN to | ~~come back~~ | + + + from | the
   un | der world
The one | who take | life do | not seize | he… | the one | who make |
   you sick | do not | seize he | ~~the un~~ | ~~der world~~ | ~~seize he~~

The min | ister | of the | god of | the un | der world | do not | seize
he | the cry | of the | earth come | up a | bout he
He do | not fall | ~~in the~~ | ~~field of~~ | ~~battle~~ | the earth | seize he

Then DIC | TATOR | son of | the wild | cow cry | + + + ~~for~~ | ~~he friend~~
| WILDMAN

To the | House of | the Dead | + + + to | the war | god he | go one |
man on | he own
'Father | war god | + + + on the | day I | ~~drop I~~ | ~~ball and~~ | ~~stick~~ in | to
the | under | world
and the | ball fall | in to | the earth
WILDMAN | who go | down to | bring it | back ~~be~~ | ~~seize by~~ | the un |
der world'

## Stone XII Cut iii

'The ~~one~~ | ~~who take~~ | ~~life~~ do | not seize | he… | the one | who make |
you sick | do not | seize he | the un | der world | seize he
The min | ister | of the | god of | the un | der world | ~~do not~~ | ~~seize he~~
| + + + the | cry of | the earth | catch hold | of he
He do | not fall | + + + on | the bat | tle field | the ~~earth~~ | ~~seize he~~'

The + + + | war god | ~~answer~~ | he word | with a | silence

DICTA | TOR go | to the | moon god | + + + one | man ~~by~~ | ~~he self~~
'Father | + + + moon | god on | the day | I drop | I ball | and I | stick
in | the un | der world
and the | ~~ball fall~~ | in to | the earth
WILDMAN | who go | down to | bring it | back be | seize by | the un |
der world
~~The one~~ | ~~who take~~ | ~~life~~ + + + | do not | seize he | the one | who
make | you sick | do not | seize he | the un | der world | seize he
The min | ister | of the | god of | the ~~un~~ | ~~der world~~ | do not | + + +
seize | he the | cry of | the earth | ~~catch hold~~ | of he
He do | not fall | + + + on | the bat | tle field | the earth | seize he'

The + + + | moon god | ~~answer~~ | he word | with a | silence

DICTA | TOR go | to the | sky god | AN one | man ~~by~~ | ~~he self~~
'Father | + + + sky | god on | the day | I drop | I ball | and I | stick in |
the un | der world
and the | ~~ball fall~~ | in to | the earth

WILDMAN | who go | down to | bring it | back be | seize by | the un |
    der world
~~The one~~ | ~~who take~~ | ~~life~~ + + + | do not | seize he | the one | who
    make | you sick | do not | seize he | the un | der world | seize he
The min | ister | of the | god of | the ~~un~~ | ~~der world~~ | do not | + + +
    seize | he the | cry of | the earth | ~~catch hold~~ | of he
He do | not fall | + + + on | the bat | tle field | the earth | seize he'

The sky | god AN | ~~answer~~ | he word | with a | silence

He go | to the | god of | knowledge | ~~one man~~ | by he | self…
'Father | god of | knowledge | on the | day I | drop I | ~~ball and~~ | ~~I stick~~
    | in the | + + + un | der world
and the | ball fall | in to | the earth
WILDMAN | who go | down to | bring it | back ~~be~~ | ~~seize by~~ | ~~the un~~ |
    ~~der world~~
The ~~one~~ | ~~who take~~ | ~~life~~ + + + | do not | seize he | the one | who
    make | you sick | do not | seize he | the un | der world | ~~seize he~~
The min | ister | of the | god of | the un | der world | do not | seize he
    | … the | cry of | the earth | ~~catch hold~~ | ~~of he~~
He do | not fall | on the | battle | + + + field | the earth | seize he'

When he | hear this | the god | of know | ledge + + + | the one | who
    make | with he | word what | be not | ~~before~~
say to | the god | of the | under | world the | ~~battle~~ | ~~hard~~…
'Listen | god of | the un | der world | battle | hard one!
~~Open~~ | ~~up a~~ | ~~hole~~ to | the un | der world
that the | shade of | WILDMAN | can is | sue from | the dark
and tell | the way | of the | ~~under~~ | ~~world~~ + + + | to he | brother'

The god | of the | under | world the | battle | hard lis | ten to | he
   word
He at | once op | en up | ~~a hole~~ | + + + to | the un | der world
The + + + | shade of | WILDMAN | issue | from the | dark like |
   a dream* (?)                                                    *or 'spirit'
They try | ~~to hold~~ | each oth | er to | kiss each | other
like DAN | TE and | CASEL | LA + + +
They trade | word cry | out to | each oth | er…

# Stone XII Cut iv

'Tell it | straight friend
tell DIC | TATOR | the + + + | way of | the un | der world'

'I will | ~~not tell~~ | ~~you man~~ | I will | not tell | you what | I see
If I | must tell | you the | way of | the un | der world | ~~get rea~~ | ~~dy to~~ |
    ~~sit down~~ | ~~and cry~~'

'I will | sit down | ~~and cry~~'

'I bo | dy that | make you | heart + + + | happy | to touch
ani | mal ~~eat~~ | ~~it all~~ | ~~up~~ like | horse meat
I bo | dy that | make you | + + + heart | happy | to touch
+ + + turn | ~~to dirt~~'

DICTA | TOR cry | out and | throw he | self to | the earth
he throw | he self | in the | + + + dirt | and say
'Do you | see the | + + + man | ~~who have~~ | no son?'
                              'I do
He.........................................'

'The one | with one | son do | you see | this man?'
                              'I do
He lie | under | the wall | and he | cry ~~tear~~ | ~~of pain~~'

'The one | with two | son do | you see | this man?'
                              'I do
He live | in a | house of | brick and | he eat | white bread.'

'~~The one~~ | ~~with~~ three | son do | you see | this one?'

                         'I do

He drink | spring wa | ter out | of a | deep well | from a | plastic |
   bottle* (?)'                                        *or 'water skin'


'The one | with four | son do | you see | this man?'

                         'I do

He heart | sing…'


'The one | with ~~five~~ | ~~son do~~ | ~~you see~~ | ~~this man~~?'

                         'I do

Like one | who write | well like | a judge | in court | every | one lis |
   ten to | he word'


'The one | with six | son do | you see | this man?'

                         'I do

Like the | man ~~who~~ | ~~drive the~~ | sport ut | ilit | y ve | hicle | across |
   the + + + | field he | stand tall'


'The one | with + + + | seven | son do | you see | this man?'

                         'I do

Like a | rock star | ~~he~~…'

## Stone XII Cut v

'Like a | flag so | bright it | ~~make you~~ | ~~blind~~ he | + + + + + +

Like + + + + + + + + + + + + + + + + + + + + +

+ + + + + + + + +...............................

..............................................

................................................

...........................................

..........................+ + + + + + + + + + + +

............................................

.......................................

.......................................

+ + + + + + + + +......................................

...............................................

.............................................

.........................................

.......................................

...............................................'

'The one | who sell | the ref | ugee | in to | the sex | trade + + + | do
    you | see this | man + + + ?'

                                    'I do

He drink | salt wat | er + + + | + + + he | eat dog | food for | he sup |
    per + + +'


'The one | who fill | the boat | with too | many | people | have you |
    set eye | on he?'

                                    'I have

For that | + + + + + + | they will | ~~tear out~~ | ~~he nail~~'

## Stone XII Cut vi

'The one | who die | all of | a sud | den* (?) do | you see | this man?'

*or 'of a bad heart'

'~~I do~~

He sleep | at night | on a | … ~~soft~~ | bed and | drink pure | water'

'The one | who give | shelter | to the | refug | ee in | he house | + + +
do | you see | this man?

'I do

He sleep | well at | night and | never | go hun | gry + + +'

'The one | ~~cut down~~ | ~~in bat~~ | ~~tle~~ do | you see | this man?'

'I do

He fat | her raise | up he | head + + + | and he | wife look | after | he
dead | body'

'The neigh | bour who | become | angry | when a | tree grow | over |
he fence | + + + + + + | do you | see this | + + + man?'

'I do

In the | under | world he | live in | darkness | he drink | dirty | water |
from an | out side | toilet'

'The one | they throw | ~~on to~~ | ~~the waste~~ | ~~land~~ do | you see | this
man?'

'I do

He spi | rit do | not + + + | rest in | peace in | the un | der world'

'The shade | who have | no one | left in | the world | to love | … do |
   you see | this one?'

                              'I do

The ~~left~~ | ~~over~~ | ~~pota~~ | ~~to~~ the | left ov | er + + + | burger | bun that |
   people | throw in | the dirt
[that no | dead dog | will touch]
he eat'

# Key

+ + + = text missing

… = untranslatable

[ ] = interpolation

~~abc~~ = partially defaced

(?) = variant reading

\* \* \* = section of tablet lost

(!) = pun

# Afterword

Translating *Gilgamesh* 'translexically' using the 1,500-word vocabulary of Globish (from the words 'global' and 'English') compiled by Jean-Paul Nerrière for use in the international business community, and which he considered the world dialect of the third millenium, may at first glance look like a peculiar and arbitrary thing to do. On one level it is, but on another there is a logic of repetition here which takes us back to the very origins of *Gilgamesh* itself.

Generally speaking translators of *Gilgamesh* can be divided into those who know cuneiform and those who don't, but whichever kind of translator we are dealing with there are two common tendencies. Firstly, as new excavations and chance discoveries unearth fresh clay tablets in cuneiform, there's an urge to increasingly fill in gaps in the story where previously lines, or sometimes whole sections of the poem, were missing. So Andrew George in his Penguin edition of the poem can write: 'In time the holes that pepper the standard version of the epic will undoubtedly be filled by further discoveries of tablets in the ruin-mounds of Mesopotamia and in the museums of the world.' Secondly, there's a tendency to translate not into anything that anyone would recognise as living English, but into a kind of bland 'translatese', a very formal, flat, neutral and unidiomatic English, sometimes one with a hectoring Victorian stamp as if directly transmitted from the era in which the tablets were first discovered by our colonialist ancestors.

One can take issue with both these tendencies. Firstly, it is quite possible to see the fragmentary nature of *Gilgamesh* as an integral and fascinating part of its material (and arguably symbolic) existence – one which, as the easily damaged clay tablets continue to be damaged in regional conflicts today, links the history of this ancient text to the history of the present, the dislocations of the text finding their counterpart in our own dislocated times. This was brought home to me in 2017 when I was involved with *Stories in Transit* working with refugees in Palermo on an adaptation of *Gilgamesh*, combining acting and puppets and animation, where many of the scenes, in particular the crossing of the sea of death, found resonance with the young participants' own experiences. Secondly, it could be argued that while we don't know for certain the register of *Gilgamesh*, there is, given the nature of its content (often violent, mocking and sexually explicit), no reason to assume that it should be translated into the elevated language that is appropriate, say, for Virgilian epic, and nothing to say that it shouldn't be translated into an idiomatic language closer to that of, say, François Villon. We can get some inkling of what this line of thinking might begin to look like when applied to *Gilgamesh*, from the little-known fragments completed by Charles Olson, which he calls 'Bigmans', which are both idiomatic and pay homage to the fragmentary nature of the epic by maintaining gaps:

> arouse yrself, Bigmans,
> arouse
>
> cities, things
> crumples
> of tin, And dead men
> in
>
> Bigmans, start

moving, start
the next heave, leave
your mother's fire: your brothers
have had enough derisions
despitous, of many filths
though fructuous

Take to the streets, Bigmans,
to the streets, go
to the whore, begin:
she is sib, wrong boy


My own version, then, begins with the decision, firstly, to maintain
rather than to disguise the fragmentary nature of the poem (the text of
*Gilgamesh* by John Gardner and John Maier, which translates the Akka-
dian version by the poet Sîn-leqi-unninni, maintaining the gaps, has
been particularly helpful here) and, secondly, to avoid the formal, flat
and neutral style that is common in translations here (Olson's drafts,
in this respect, are the exception that proves the rule). And yet, the
question remains, what kind of language should one translate *Gilgamesh*
into? This is difficult, if not impossible, to answer, as the truth is that
we don't really know how the original would have read. Any decision
to use one particular idiom over another, therefore, risks being arbi-
trary. And yet, there is some evidence for the use of idiomatic language
in the poem. Benjamin R. Foster, for example, in the Norton edition
notes that while tone and usage in such an ancient text are 'hazardous
topics', that in Tablet VI, line 72, Isullanu, the gardener, appears to use
non-standard forms which could be translated either as archaic and
proverbial ('Hath my mother not baked?') or as a colloquialism ('Hain't
my mother baked?'). As often with my own writing, it was the Oulipo

which suggested a possible solution, and that solution was to make use of a constraint, namely the idea of translating into the limited vocabulary of Globish, a technique Oulipo call translexical translation, here involving translation from the lexicon of standard English into that of Globish. Constraints are at their most effective when they are not arbitrary but are underpinned by some aesthetic rationale (as with Georges Perec's 'e'-less novel *La disparition*), yet as Globish is primarily a business language it is entirely appropriate to use this to translate a text originally written in cuneiform which itself, as a script, emerged from the need to record business transactions: so many bushels of wheat, so many jars of wine. Moreover, just as Jean-Paul Nerrière considered Globish the world dialect of the third millenium, so Akkadian, the language of the standard text for *Gilgamesh*, as in R. Campbell Thompson's standard text established in 1930, was for a long time the *lingua franca* of international communications in the Near East. You can get a good sense of the business orientation of Globish from its first twenty words: an, able, about, above, accept, accident, *account*, across, act, *add*, *administration*, admit, adult, *advertise*, *advise*, after, again, against, *agency*, *aggression*. Worth noting in passing is the coincidence that the first word in Globish, 'An', is also the Sumerian name for the sky god who appears in the epic, and therefore the only god that can be mentioned by name. The link between script and language and business, crucially, is also there in the substance of the epic, for here – as with other epics like the *Iliad*, as Crista Wolf has argued, or as with *The Táin*, where events are precipitated by the theft of a bull – there is an underpinning theme involving trade, here the trade in hard wood (or, according to some, pine) and access to forests for building materials (something which, again, links this epic to more recent wars in and around Iraq, where the commodity in question has not been wood, but oil).

One result of this approach, because of the limited vocabulary of

Globish, was the use of periphrasis, so 'Uruk-the-Sheepfold', for example, became 'big city of the animal noise', the 'Bull of Heaven' became 'the MAN COW of the sky' and so on. The centrality of the Bull of Heaven to the narrative, as well as the centrality of issues linked to male virility, suggest that this is not only our earliest epic, but our earliest cock and bull story too. The limitations of Globish made other things difficult to translate directly, too, so that often there was a necessary updating (a bit like doing Shakespeare in contemporary dress) with the substitution of contemporary or anachronistic terms (such as 'nuclear', 'rocket', 'helicopter', 'chemical weapon', 'magazine', 'car', 'sport utility vehicle', 'cell phone', 'brand', 'retirement', or 'hard hat') and here the substitution resembled more the operation of the dream-work than conventional one-to-one translation. As a result the final text frequently has a sense of the clash of the ancient and the modern, a clash which is not inappropriate in a text about cultural encounters (notably between culture and the wild), and it also incorporates a clash of different registers, moving between formal and informal – not that Globish itself is particularly idiomatic, it is not, but its vocabulary can be subverted and used to string together sentences and phrases that are, e.g., 'get with', 'spit it out', 'throw up' and 'face it'. This particular quality emerged almost by chance, like a spark, though it is in some ways typical of writing that uses a limited vocabulary, but it was a quality that I teased out when I could. The appropriateness of this clash of registers to a version of Gilgamesh in particular is confirmed by Marina Warner writing in the LRB when she says that in 1872 George Smith 'delivered a paper to the Society for Biblical Archaeology, and read out the account of the flood from the epic. This was the first time the Epic of Gilgamesh had been heard and understood after an interval of two thousand years: the longest sleep ever among the world's great poems [...] The work's interrupted chronology, so different from the destinies of the *Upanishads* or even Homer, gives *Gilgamesh* a double history, as an ancient epic and as a modern narrative poem.'

Finally, a word on the metre of *Gilgamesh*. According to Andrew George, because of the variable nature of the sign in cuneiform – some signs for example, are syllabic, whereas some represent complete words – line length, defined by the width of the tablet column, is extremely variable when translated. The line can comprise three, four, five or even six units, and each of these units in themselves while having a central word can be markedly variable in syllabic length. To adopt a metaphor, the line might be said to be explosive, and like a cluster bomb the exact number of explosions is unpredictable. On the one hand this arrangement gives a highly flexible line, as in free-verse, on the other hand it maintains a structure, in that it is built up of discrete units. In this respect, it is a remarkably modern metric, in that like Mallarmé's *Un coup de dés*, as Quentin Meillassoux has argued, it squares the circle of free and fixed verse forms. To achieve a similar end I adopted a flexible line, sometimes short, though frequently longer, which owes something to the lines of Anne Carson, combined with an arrangement I had found in the work of the poet Richard Parker, where the line is divided into two-syllable units with a vertical bar, often cutting words in half. Used in translating *Gilgamesh* this practice had the added benefit of invoking the ghostly presence of cuneiform in its angularity, and also increased a sense of the fragmentary while adding a new level of uncertainty and unfamiliarity to the decipherment of the line, thereby enacting a kind of 'restrangement', taking us back to the moment of the first encounter with this strange and foreign script, when George Smith, visiting the British Museum in his lunch hour to peer at the flood tablets, slowly began to work out how to *read* them.

Philip Terry